# OVERCOMING ADDICTION

A

COMMMON

SENSE

APPROACH

Michael Hardiman

THE CROSSING PRESS
FREEDOM, CALIFORNIA

© 2000 Michael Hardiman
Cover and interior design by Courtnay Perry
Printed in the USA
Second Printing, 2001

First published in 1998 by Newleaf, an imprint of Gill and Macmillan, Ltd., Goldenbridge, Dublin 8

**Cautionary Note:** The information contained within this book is in no way intended as a substitute for medical counseling. Please do not attempt self-treatment of a medical problem without consulting a qualified health practitioner.

The author and The Crossing Press expressly disclaim any and all liability for any claims, damages, losses, judgements, expenses, costs, and liabilities of any kind or injuries resulting from any products offered in this book by participating companies and their employees or agents. Nor does the inclusion of any resource group or company listed within this book constitute an endorsement or guarantee of quality by the author or The Crossing Press.

For information on bulk purchases or group discounts for this and other Crossing Press titles, please contact our Sales Manager at 800/777-1048.

Visit our website on the Internet: **www.crossingpress.com**

### Library of Congress Cataloging-in-Publication Data

Hardiman, Michael.
    Overcoming addiction : the common sense approach / by Michael Hardiman.
      p. cm.
   ISBN 1-58091-013-0 (pbk.)
    1. Substance abuse.  2. Addicts—Psychology.  3. Addicts—Rehabilitation.  I. Title.

   HV4998.H37     2000
   362.29—dc21                     99-057493

# TABLE OF CONTENTS

# FOREWORD

An innate desire to live life with the least amount of pain and the greatest amount of pleasure leaves each person vulnerable to addiction. For many, the reality of their lives is painful. Difficulties in relationships, insecurities, poverty, social isolation, personal unhappiness, and the pressures of modern living—all foster a mental tendency to deny or escape the awareness of pain and discomfort. This book is a very valuable resource for all those ill-informed about the nature of addiction, the extraordinary ease with which individuals become imprisoned by it, and its complex passage of distortion and destruction in the lives of both those who become addicted and of their families.

Its publication is important because it makes simple and accessible what is generally considered to be a very complex issue. The author, Michael Hardiman, addresses the subject of addiction with great sensitivity, clarity, and thoroughness. He also reaches into the heart of the matter to bear witness to the struggle and suffering of those addicted.

The importance of recognizing the unique nature of, and meaning expressed in, each person's addiction, is very well elaborated. So too are the physical and psychological aspects of addiction, as well as the nature of the spiritual quest, and the yearnings and longing for connection and bliss that drive individuals towards the "rewards" of alcohol and drugs.

Hardiman explores and examines some of the options for

recovery, from self-help programs to the more specialized treatments, with a wide range of recovery options. This book is a clear statement that the care of those addicted should not be the preserve of a few specialists. It offers information and guidance on a wide range of recovery options.

This book should prove a reliable and readable resource for the layperson as well as professionals.

MAURA RUSSELL
Director, The Rutland Centre
Templeogue, Dublin

# CHAPTER I

# What Is Addiction?

It is understandable that some people despise addicts as weak-willed folks who can't look after themselves and at the same time dismiss those who try to help addicts as naive idealists. Is this simple view accurate? Is it merely a matter of some people failing to control certain activities and causing great harm as a result, or is there some more complex process at work? It is time to ask the question, "What is addiction?"

The term comes from the Latin ad *dicere,* which means "to give oneself up," or "to give oneself over to another power." Addiction occurs when persons surrender to a substance or activity, which gradually takes control of their life and eventually destroys them if they do not recover. The fact that addiction is an enslavement to some substance or activity is generally accepted by those who are caregivers for addicts. What is still debated is the manner in which persons become enslaved. Why do some people become addicts and others do not? Why do some recover, while others eventually die as a direct or indirect result of their addiction? Why do some addicts spend their lives struggling between abstaining and relapsing?

There appear to be four main components to any addiction, namely compulsion, dependence, regularity, and destructiveness.

Each of these becomes more and more extreme, as addiction expands and develops in the life of the addict.

A compulsion is a very strong, sometimes overwhelming, desire to do something. In some cases, this turns out to be true: the addicted individual feels an intense desire to use a drug, or act out the addictive behavior.

Dependence is the *need* to do something, as distinct from a *desire* to do it. Central to this notion is relying on someone or something. Dependence, as it relates to addiction, is the knowledge or belief that some negative or undesirable result will follow if the person does not take drugs, or act out an addictive behavior.

Regularity means that the addictive behavior is a consistent feature of the person's life. There can be a great deal of variation among people in terms of the number of addictive events. One alcoholic may go on a binge every six months, whereas another may drink everyday. The number of addictive events may change as the addiction grows in strength, so what may have begun as a weekly, or fortnightly, event may become a daily occurrence.

There are varied degrees of destructiveness, from ongoing gradual deterioration to catastrophic injury, and a wide range of possibilities in between.

Combining these elements, we can reach a definition of addiction as a condition whereby an individual regularly takes a substance, or acts in a particular way, in response to a strong and sometimes overwhelming desire to do so; and that in the absence of so doing, he will experience negative feelings or actual illness. By taking the substance or carrying out the behavior, the addict causes harm to himself or to others.

Using this definition, addicts are involved in doing something that is harmful to themselves or others in response to a strong desire and a fear of what will happen if they don't. This approach implies that addicts are not simply irresponsible people, but that they are responding to very strong driving forces behind their addictive behaviors.

Furthermore, it implies that addiction is not an all-or-nothing phenomenon. It is impossible to draw a line between addiction and non-addiction. In general, becoming addicted is a gradual process, measured by the intensity of the compulsion, the depth of dependence, and the degree of destructiveness. Thus, one person can be mildly addicted to something, whereas another can be very strongly addicted to the same thing. The intensity of addiction is often related to the nature of the substance or activity, and the length of time the individual has been involved with it.

It is clear that everybody is a potential addict, and maybe most of us are in some way involved in addictive behavior. Some addictions are much more destructive than others, and some people progress far down the road of the more dangerous addictions. It is these people who destroy their own lives and damage others whom we tend to identify as true addicts.

To help treat and heal these lives, and minimize the damage, it is important to understand the four main parts of addiction:

1. the nature of the driving forces that produce addiction;

2. the psychological states of the addicted person;

3. the variety of addictive substances or behaviors;

4. the process by which recovery occurs.

The remainder of this book addresses these issues.

# CHAPTER II

# The Causes of Addiction

Much controversy has surrounded this topic over the past few decades. Some view addiction as a disease that overtakes some people, but not others—a kind of genetic time bomb, that lies dormant within the make-up of the addict until it is triggered by ingesting a chemical. Psychologists and social workers tend to emphasize the social and psychological aspects of addiction, seeing it as a response to emotional dysfunction or social impoverishment. Those with a religious focus may see it as moral failure and the basic sinfulness of humankind. In this chapter I try to explain why certain people become addicted while others do not. There is no one cause for addiction—looking for a single cause to such a complex, widespread human phenomenon is pointless.

Addiction is fast becoming the main social health care issue of modern society. Every generation has had a key social health problem. At the turn of the century, there was destitution wrought by urbanization and the industrial revolution. Disease was rampant in densely populated slums, where bad hygiene, little medicine, and an uncaring elite left thousands to their fate. Two world wars in a forty-year period cost millions of lives and destroyed many European countries, making it difficult to see any social health trend developing until the peaceful era of the 1950s. Since then, with economic expansion, the problem of addiction has grown and spread throughout most Western societies. Addiction is like a cancer spreading throughout the human family, and like cancer, it will take a lot of research to prevent its spread and to treat those afflicted. If we know the causes of addiction, then we can begin to look for solutions.

Gordon Allport, one of the founding fathers of psychology, offered a brilliant insight into human behavior with the term "functional autonomy." By this he means that some human behavior can be caused by a set of forces or events, but the behavior can continue for reasons other than those that gave rise to it in the first place. I think this notion is vital to understanding the link between the causes of addiction and the forces that keep addiction going. The original causes may not be the forces that sustain addiction. Thus, there are two distinct dimensions, the original causes and the sustaining forces.

There are at least three key elements involved in why people become addicted:

1. the nature of the addicting substance;

2. the powerful motivation behind some people's need to alter their internal emotional experience, or to put it more simply, to change their mood artificially;

3. the individual's physical vulnerability to addictive substances.

The beginning of all addiction is a combination of these three elements. Let's look at each of them more closely.

Certain substances are powerfully addictive, and we need look no further than the exposure to the substance itself to explain why a person becomes addicted. These substances affect the body chemistry, usually the central nervous system, leading to a mood change. How addictive they are depends on several things—the speed at which they affect the body chemistry, the way the body adapts to their presence, the experience they produce, and the speed at which they leave the body. Substances that act quickly and are quick to leave the body are the most addictive. Nicotine, for example, is so highly addictive that we need not look elsewhere for the cause of cigarette smoking. Most people try cigarette smoking as teenagers. After a few initial upsets—coughing, dizziness, nausea—the body adapts and the individual becomes quickly hooked to the stimulant drug, nicotine. The drug enters the bloodstream via the lungs and goes quickly to the brain. It takes about thirty minutes to start clearing from the system, which leads to withdrawal pangs and a desire to smoke again. This is why many people smoke an average of twenty cigarettes a day.

Other addictions are not so easily understood. Human beings desire pleasure and avoid pain. Many activities make us feel good. Eating, sex, rest, and exercise are all basic physical activities that provide pleasures. Achievement, praise, and affection are psychological equivalents. Conversely, painful experiences often accompany dangerous events or behaviors. Getting too close to an open fire causes a mild burning sensation, which helps us to avoid a serious burn. Going too long without food causes hunger pangs. Not enough love produces a feeling of loneliness. These painful experiences help us to avoid danger and to seek what we need to be healthy. Every human being is, therefore, to some extent, pursuing pleasure and avoiding pain. Addiction is a good example of what happens when this process becomes distorted or unbalanced.

Addicts in general begin by using some substance or behavior in an inappropriate way to produce pleasure or avoid pain, thus affecting their emotional state. The kinds of experience sought after are many and varied, but they have one thing in common: a desire to repeat the experience. There are four kinds of such experience:

1. creating a feeling of elation or excitement

2. relieving anxiety or some other emotional distress

3. creating a feeling of power or confidence

4. creating a feeling of connection or unity

Let us examine each in turn.

I remember the day at a soccer game when our team won and we congratulated each other in a pure, unrestrained expression of joy and exhilaration. It was a very exciting experience that gave me an inkling of the seductive attraction of an event or substance.

Certain chemicals (mainly stimulants) and certain activities (e.g., compulsive gambling), can produce feelings of great elation and pleasure. It is easy to understand the temptation to repeat such activities. People enslaved to the need for elation or excitement are one particular set of addicts. They often have difficulties with responsibility and have a low tolerance for endurance. They tend to be a somewhat immature in their development. They differ from those people who use drugs or addictive behavior to ease and repress painful feelings. This leads to a very important observation about addiction. Every addict has a particular preference for certain substances. The drug of choice is determined by the kind of experience sought. Thus, there are many reasons why certain addicts are attracted to particular kinds of experiences. Taking account of these reasons is an essential element in assisting long-term recovery for addicts.

The second type of mood alteration is that of relieving painful feelings. A very common cause of addiction is the use of chemicals or addictive behavior to relieve emotional pain. Prescription drugs such as Valium and other sedative chemicals including alcohol are more often the choice when this is the underlying purpose. Addictive activities such as self-mutilation and eating disorders are also related to a need to relieve internal emotional pain. The world for many people offers no opportunity for improvement. Long-term unemployment leaves a sense of betrayal and boredom. Many do not have the skills to change their lives. Along comes a drug that can be bought legally and a place where it can be drunk; where the dart board, the pool table, and the camaraderie all combine to relieve boredom, to enhance warm feelings of connection to others, to relieve feelings of helplessness and desperation. It is easy to understand the seductive power of this drug, and why so many fall foul to its ministrations and become addicts.

This is only one of many possible images that illustrate the point that many addicts are trying to relieve some kind of pain. They unfortunately end up dependent on a substance that can only makes things worse, which in turn increases the need for the drug. Thus, the crippling cycle—pain, relief or escape, more pain, more relief—continues until finally destruction follows. This is common in many forms of addiction.

Psychologist Alfred Adler considered that the need for power is a fundamental driving force in people. Much of my experience suggests that he is correct. There are many meanings of the word power. Here it refers to the ability to exert influence on the course of one's life. Without some sense of power, we become helpless pawns, pushed hither and thither, dominated and used for other people's ends. I have been fascinated at the way many powerless people become fodder for those who exert power.

Childhood experiences can influence why a person becomes powerless. This sense of powerlessness may be revealed in adult life in the following ways: being unable to solve problems and to create an individual life; being attracted to people who can be depended upon for direction; being unable to make decisions for oneself; and being unable to leave situations that are hurtful or damaging.

Lack of initiative is rooted in the belief that nothing a person does will make any difference. People like this feel that life happens to them. They take little responsibility and are often directionless. Instead of developing into adults who know what they wish to do with their lives, they sit back and let somebody else make decisions for them. They are drawn to people who like to take control. Early on, there is comfort in having someone, or some system of belief, to give them direction on how to live. Eventually, this leads to a growing sense of helplessness. To live healthy and fulfilling lives, we must be able to exert some degree of power over our environment. Those who become powerless are almost always damaged by the experience.

Into this context let us introduce a drug, such as cocaine or another hallucinogen that gives a feeling of superiority, omnipotence, and/or a deep feeling of being in control. When such drugs wear off, the feelings of powerlessness, the attendant fear and anxiety become even greater, and may even become more extreme. This often leads to cross addiction. An individual might use, for example, an opiate such as heroin to help cope with the emotional crash from drugs that are used to produce feelings of power, and then gradually become addicted to the second drug, heroin.

Thus far we have discussed drugs in relation to emotional needs. Another set of needs that often underlies the use of certain drugs or activities may belong to the spiritual realm, namely the relation to the cosmos. Altered states of consciousness are common. These occur when people's awareness of the here and now becomes overtaken by internal experiences usually of a dramatic nature. This can be described as unity consciousness. At such times, many individuals claim to have met God, or to have had an experience of becoming one with the universe. Such people have lost their sense of identity, but have gained an overriding sense of peace, and a feeling that they are part of a great purpose.

Such people have been called mystics. Techniques such as meditation, breathing, drumming, and repetition of mantras were used, sometimes along with drugs, to enhance these experiences. In general, the individuals who embarked on these journeys to the interior realms of the soul were held in respect and awe by others in the community. The altered states of consciousness had an important role in the overall spiritual welfare of the community at large.

Today, altered states of consciousness have lost their cultural and religious mooring. Additionally, more and more chemicals are available that can create this state quickly for people who take them. Alongside these changes, the growing materialistic and consumer-driven ethos has lessened the importance of the sacred and elevated the secular. Orthodox religions have lost much of their credibility, and are therefore less able to direct the spiritual growth of those in their care. These changes have left an enormous spiritual vacuum.

Some people do not understand the nature of this spiritual crisis. Perhaps all they experience is a deep sense of ennui, or alienation. Into this widespread spiritual hunger they bring hallucinogenic substances, or opiates, or some well-packaged meditative technique. The scene is then set for many people to be seduced into a counterfeit spirituality that leaves them ultimately spiritually bankrupt, physically injured, and in many cases emotionally destroyed.

Some people seem to be more prone to chemical addiction than others. This vulnerability to addiction is related to the way their brain chemistry interacts with addictive substances and may be genetically inherited. There is a continuing search for medication to treat the chemistry of the brain, so as to reduce or get rid of its need for addictive substances. Presently, there are drugs on the market—or that are being developed—that treat the craving for alcohol, nicotine, heroin, and cocaine.

There is a physical component in addiction. Chemical addiction is profoundly physical in nature. The question is whether or not the addiction is physically dormant within the person, awaiting the ingesting of a substance that sets off its progress. Can a person be an addict before they take a drug? Is a person an alcoholic before taking a drink? There is, in my opinion, no definitive answer to this question. Certain people, who inherit a vulnerability to addiction, never become addicts; others, with no family or genetic tendency, can and do become addicted. And, as we saw earlier, taking certain drugs will lead to addiction no matter what physical or psychological forces are at work. The best we can do is accept that statistically, more people with a physical vulnerability to addiction will become addicted than will those who do not have such a vulnerability.

# CHAPTER III

# What Sustains Addiction?

Early attempts to understand addiction led to the conclusion that there was a certain personality type that could be called an addictive personality; people who were considered to be emotionally immature, easily frustrated, low in willpower, and generally irresponsible. There was a serious flaw in this approach, however. Much of what was seen as part of the personality of addicts was a symptom of the addiction, rather than its cause. This realization led to a closer study of the personality changes that may occur as a result of addiction: falling in love, building defenses, chasing the dragon, and moral deterioration.

Perhaps no experience is as dramatic in its effect as that wonderfully strange and often anguished experience of falling in love. I saw this recently in my work. A young woman, who was quite troubled with her family, came to see me a number of times for help with her problems. Her face was mask-like, and she spoke of her most difficult problems in the same flat tone as the most ordinary events. She never smiled. I kept trying to help her express herself and let some of her feelings come to the surface. Then one day, she arrived and I could see that despite her usual timidity and defensiveness, something had changed. She gradually revealed the cause; she had met a young man and was falling for him. Each time she mentioned his name, a smile lit up her features—she became animated and expressive. It reminded me strongly of seeing this effect in a completely different context, that of addiction.

John came to see me soon after discharge from a psychiatric hospital, where he had been treated for severe alcoholism, which, over fifteen years, had almost completely destroyed him. During one session, I asked him to describe the first time he drank. His voice changed, and a softness crept into his face. He held up an imaginary glass and I believe that he could see, in his mind's eye, the light reflecting off a bronze liquid. After a brief moment of quiet reflection, he described the feeling, first encountered through alcohol, when he "tasted the elixir of life."

Falling in love is an incredibly intense happiness of coming home to a place that is truly warm, safe, and delightful, one that seems to meet all your needs and heal all your hurts. John's recollection of that first drink is comparable to that experience. This nostalgia and sentiment, common among addicts, is called "euphoric recall." Addicts fall in love with their drug of choice and build a very strong emotional attachment to it.

When we fall in love, certain changes occur, including changes to the chemistry of the brain. We go slightly insane. Our thoughts become obsessive and we think of the loved one constantly; we miss them when they are away, and we look forward to the wonderful times ahead, of sharing, loving, holding, and healing. Work and friendships may be neglected as finally unimportant. We idealize the loved one and are unable to see any faults. We are intrigued and charmed by their little idiosyncrasies (which with the passage of time we will grow to dislike, even resent). And we are loyal to that person, so much so that no one will be allowed to question the newfound love. The fact that he is broke, angry with the world, irresponsible, ruthless, or changeable has no bearing on our love and our belief that this is it: we have found the one. Likewise, the addict, in falling in love with his substance, has found something to rely on that will make his world better and release him from his struggle. He protects this experience from the cold criticism of others by building a psychological defense structure.

The next personality change occurs when the addict's life begins to come apart as a direct result of his addiction. These negative consequences cause some readjustments to occur in the psyche of the addict. Eliot Aronson, a social psychologist, discovered what most of us know intuitively—that human beings cannot live comfortably while holding two incompatible beliefs. This is called "cognitive dissonance." This refers to the anxiety that occurs when we are faced with two of our beliefs that contradict each other.

Let us look at a few examples. Some people have expectations based on prophecies that the world as we know it will come to an end. Many have traveled out to remote places to watch the apocalypse, only to have to drive home disappointed. Their sacred scriptures and leaders, inspired by God, told them it would happen—but it didn't. One belief, inspired by God, is dissonant with the other, "God was wrong." Addiction creates one of the most intense forms of cognitive dissonance, namely: how can a substance or activity I love so much, need so badly, and depend on so heavily, be so bad for me? In coping with this conflict, many addicts go through major changes in personality. To understand addiction and recovery, we need to examine these changes.

Aronson's work is useful to explain why addicts go to such lengths to defend themselves. Freudian psychology, on the other hand, explains how the addict raises such defenses. Combining these two approaches, we can see that addicts develop an elaborate, distorted way of seeing things that allows them to withstand the anxiety and pain of facing up to the effects of their addiction. This distorted system is constructed by using several defense mechanisms.

Freud recognized that defense mechanisms were a part of normal personality functioning. They are often important tools in coping with difficult and traumatic situations. They can give people sufficient time to come to terms with a problem and become psychologically prepared for change. They become problematic, however, when people consistently rely on them in order to block out reality.

In cases of addiction, defense mechanisms become an intrinsic part of the addictive process. The defense mechanisms used by addicts are no different from those used by most people, but they are used in a dysfunctional manner. Several key defense mechanisms that occur in most addictions are denial, rationalization, minimization, projection, and displacement.

Denial is the "belle of the ball" of defense mechanisms. It can be defined as the inability to see a problem as real. It is not simply a matter of lying to oneself or to others (although lying can be part of denial). Rather, it is psychological blindness. For example, denial is the initial response many people have to bereavement. The telephone rings, a person is told by a relative that their mother has died. After hanging up the telephone, the person walks around in a daze and begins to find a set of possibilities that might explain the information, other than the reality of the death. The person may live in this denial state for a short time, or may remain in it for years. In relation to bereavement, the initial purpose of denial is to help the individual prepare for the overwhelming feelings of grief that follow the loss of a loved one.

Addiction usually brings an increase in the use of denial by the addict as a defense mechanism to protect himself from the negative consequences of addiction. He does not believe there is a problem and will explain his situation away in a variety of ways. Additionally, his drug use may interfere with his perception of reality, so he may not even understand the problem.

Everyone else may see the obvious problems—ill health, missed work, wild mood changes, inappropriate and/or dangerous behavior. While the addict may deny all this, he may not even perceive the same information as others do, because of the effect of chemicals. A classic example is the alcoholic blackout. Blackouts occur when a person drinks to the point where experiences are not recorded by the brain in the normal way. Often the events that happen during the black-out period can only be recalled when the person gets intoxicated again.

"The morning after the night before" may dawn on the partner of an alcoholic as a bleak experience, as she remembers her inebriated partner ogling the hostess and making blatant sexual innuendoes. Her partner denies it, saying it wasn't so bad and all in good fun. The reality is he can't remember the event and doesn't want to admit it because it will only fuel her conviction that he has a drinking problem.

Rationalization is a common defense mechanism in which a person will give logical reasons for inappropriate behavior, a more sophisticated version of making excuses. Nobody wants to feel foolish or out of control. And most of us use rationalization as a means of protecting ourselves when we make mistakes. Let's take a very simple, everyday example. You are walking along absentmindedly and suddenly trip over yourself.

For a brief moment, you are out of control, lose your balance, and look somewhat foolish. Your immediate reaction is to look at the ground with puzzled intensity to discover what has tripped you. A large part of this is to provide yourself and on-lookers with a rational explanation for your clumsiness. In most instances, it is not a matter of the ground being at fault, but there is comfort in believing it to be so. Rationalization is quite a common and often useful method of defending one's ego.

In addiction, however, rationalization becomes extreme and very destructive, as it allows addicts to explain away many of the worst elements of their behavior. In the early stages of addiction, the reasons given for addictive behavior can have a ring of truth. The person in early-stage anorexia, for example, can give compelling reasons for losing weight. Dress size and the economics of her wardrobe, as well as the need to be healthy, can all be a reasonable facade to cover a growing obsession with food and losing weight. It can be difficult to argue with these seemingly plausible reasons for the dieting and exercising. It becomes more difficult to hear these same explanations used by an emaciated person, whose body is deteriorating from the effects of starvation.

Similarly, early-stage alcoholism comes with a fairly common set of plausible reasons. A person who drinks on the way home every night may say it helps him relax and be in better shape to tend to his family when he gets home. Another can say that drink helps him to gain confidence. A woman who works in the home may believe that her mid-morning gin and tonic gives her the energy she needs to keep house. Rationalization is primarily used, not to convince others of the reasonableness of addictive pursuits (although that is one feature), but rather to allow the addict to convince himself.

Minimization is a near relative to denial. While denial works by failure to see or acknowledge a problem, minimization works by stripping away some of the more difficult and destructive aspects of addictive behavior, leaving a not so serious problem. Look at the use of credit cards, for example. Many people buy things on credit because they are able to minimize the difficulties involved in repayment (e.g., it works out at only $10 a week). It could be said that without the use of defense mechanisms on the part of borrowers, many banks would make far less profit!

In addiction, minimization is developed to a keen level. A recent discussion with a young man heavily psychologically dependent on cannabis, whose functioning has seriously deteriorated from his drug taking, clarifies this issue. Within moments of asking whether his drug habit is related to his other difficulties, including low tolerance for frustration and almost zero motivation and energy, he minimizes the problem. He says he only smokes in the evening (neglecting to say that he doesn't go to bed until 5 a.m.). He is also quick to explain that most of his friends smoke the odd joint (neglecting to discuss one or two who are heavy users), and that furthermore, cannabis is less toxic than nicotine. It is clear that he believes that what he is doing is much less serious than it is. By minimizing his use of cannabis, he avoids making the connection between its place in his life and his other problems.

Projection and displacement are quite similar. Projection occurs when we see in other people attributes and feelings that we refuse to recognize in ourselves. At a movie, we view an image projected on a blank screen. If the film is any good, we forget that we are looking at an image and become engaged in the story. All of us, to a greater or lesser extent, project things onto other people. An angry person can easily project his anger onto others. He is obsessed by all the angry people who are out to get him. A frightened person sees danger around every corner. A confident person looks at the same corners and sees interesting opportunities. Most of us, therefore, are consistently engaged in projecting our internal emotional states onto the screen of reality.

Displacement involves taking something that is inside us and putting it where it doesn't belong. Here is a good example. A man gets into trouble at work and his boss tells him off. As a result, he is very angry with his boss and with himself, but is afraid to express his anger in case he gets into more trouble. On his arrival home he gets angry with his wife because she hasn't prepared a meal for him. She gets upset at his unfair criticism—after all, she's out working too. She recognizes that he is very touchy, so rather than escalate the conflict, she says nothing and represses her anger. Some time later, their son arrives in from play with mud on his jacket, and she yells at him. He gets upset, says nothing, goes outside, and kicks the cat. This scenario shows the defense mechanism of displacement. In each situation, the individual takes out his or her frustrations on someone who is not at fault.

In cases of addiction the person will blame others for the problems in his life that are the direct result of his drinking, drug use, etc. Most addicts are notoriously resentful, believing that the world is responsible for their unhappiness. Phrases such as "if only"—she would be nicer to me, she would give me more sex, she weren't such a nag, talk to me more, etc., etc., then I wouldn't drink, take Valium, overeat—are all classic examples of projection. In each, the individual fails to take responsibility for his own behavior and refuses to accept that his behavior is not someone else's fault. The target of projection—be it spouse, friend or relative—can end up in a living hell trying to improve so that the addict will stop complaining.

In addiction, displacement can result in violence and brutality, as the addict takes out his growing frustration on other people. Projection is essentially the act of targeting others as responsible; displacement is the next step, punishing them for being responsible. In some situations, displaced anger is expressed indirectly by the addict refusing to support his family. A teenager may use his threats to kill himself as a powerful lever to hurt his parents for imagined wrongs that have led him to fail at school or at work—when in fact it is his drinking or drugging that is at fault. These defense mechanisms can be quite subtle, but each aims to distract the addict and the people close to him from addictive behavior. A person in a relationship with an addict can be sidetracked easily if the focus is put on to their deficiencies, rather than on the addict's own behavior.

The above is a rather simplified and brief description of the more common defense mechanisms. Using some combination of these, the addict avoids reality and continues to seek the experiences that the drug, or addictive behavior, originally gave him, even as his life becomes more and more unmanageable. This illusive search for the high or fix is such a feature of addiction that it has its own name in drug folklore—chasing the dragon.

It is not helpful to speak of drugs, including illegal substances, as if they have no benefits. We know that certain drugs can make a person feel absolutely wonderful, perhaps more wonderful than any experience they might have in a drug-free state. There are no lengths to which some people will go to access these experiences. The controversial film, *Trainspotting*, suggested, for example, that the rush from a heroin fix was akin to the best orgasm a person can have, multiplied by a thousand. For the addict, however, there is a gradual change from the original wonderful experience to the desperate struggle to recreate that experience, even as the person's life becomes more and more painful. Relief from pain can be experienced as pleasurable, and here lies the seduction of some forms of addiction. The original pleasure is lost forever, but the addict doesn't realize this. In general, the addict fails to recognize that to a large extent his drug use becomes a desperate struggle to avoid the pain of withdrawal. The relief from withdrawal feels pleasurable, but it is not the pleasure of the original state, and the addict begins a futile search for an illusory first experience, one that will forever elude him.

The addicted individual becomes enslaved to a drug-created experience that he protects from the cold and painful eye of reality, while he pirouettes between the search for an illusion and the relief from pain. The dance gradually becomes a downward spiral, and the addict can become unrecognizable as the reasonable, accommodating person he once was. This leads to another feature of the progression of addiction—moral deterioration.

It has become somewhat old-fashioned to speak of morality when discussing addiction. There is a broad consensus amongst the informed that addiction is not a moral problem. This consensus emerged as a direct result of the failure of moral approaches to substance abuse—embodied, for example, in the temperance movement. Addiction came to be seen as a disorder or disease that was not responsive to moral exhortation. Morality is, however, an important element in the story of addiction, not as a punitive, guilt-inducing lever to force the addict into submission, but rather as one of the casualties of addiction.

Those who observe addicted people realize that the moral constraints that keep us safe from very destructive behavior are gradually eroded in addicts. They often behave in ways that are clearly morally wrong. It is difficult for some people to understand this progression. This difficulty arises because we tend to see morality as being a God-given function, residing in the soul, that is somewhat mysterious and less prone to corruption than other elements of personality, such as personal hygiene and good manners. There may be simpler explanations.

Psychologists now recognize that moral development and reasoning are not very different from other aspects of development. It involves a value system that emerges through the emotional bonds between a growing child and the people around him. It has two aspects—intellectual beliefs and emotional connections. Thinking and feeling are central elements of morality. These require the healthy functioning of the central nervous system. Most addictive drugs damage this system to a greater or lesser extent and thus affect the person's capacity to function in a morally healthy manner. This is the first part of why addiction damages morality. The second reason lies in the human reaction to pain.

It is common for people to react destructively when they are frightened, or in great trauma. We see evidence for this in reports of people trampled to death by a crowd of decent citizens in a state of panic trying to avoid a fire, or when people are starving and will beat or kill others for a slice of bread. The need for survival can cause ordinary people to become destructive and aggressive. When we judge those who act aggressively as a result of addiction, we tend not to believe that in similar circumstances we might fare no better. One recovering heroin addict told me that his experience of withdrawal was like having the worst toothache you could imagine. I thought this a vivid illustration, particularly having recently read an account of a man who shot off half his jaw because of a toothache. Those who do not understand the nature of withdrawal can often underestimate the degree to which most human beings would react to this kind of pain, and the desperate acts that it often produces. I believe most people would compromise some of their deeply held moral values and rob their nearest friend to avoid such pain. This explanation of the moral deterioration in addiction is unacceptable and distasteful to those who prefer to believe that addicts are somehow weaker or less moral than themselves.

# CHAPTER IV

# Signs and Symptoms

The changes that occur in an addict's personality are often matched by certain behavior patterns that can alert those around the addict. Some classic signs are mood swings, lying, stealing, unexplained absences, physical symptoms, and recurrent illness. If a number of these become consistent and seem to be out of character, they can be taken as evidence of a growing addiction. It is important to say at this point that any one of these signs can occur without a connection to addiction or substance abuse. We have to be careful not to jump to conclusions. This is particularly relevant for adolescents.

Everybody experiences mood swings, especially those people who are lively in temperament. In addiction, mood changes are generally more extreme and out of character—they seem to come out of nowhere. The highs are higher and the lows lower. The addict's eyes in particular may be dilated, he or she may look slightly dazed.

Mood swings involving anger are particularly telling. The individual may show less control and fly off the handle at the smallest thing. Physical violence and abusive language are also a consistent feature of certain addictions, such as alcohol and amphetamines. Paranoia may also be evidence of certain drug addictions—heavy marijuana usage, for example. The individual may seem very self-conscious and vigilant.

Loss of control over one's emotions is a general feature of all addiction. It is the underlying factor in mood swings. This is often due to the effect of drugs on the central nervous system. It may also result from a general increase in frustration and unhappiness.

Lying is very common, because an addict has to hide the truth from himself and others. It becomes part of the addict's lifestyle—he does things that he doesn't want others to know anything about. For example, the need for money is often vital, and the addict will make up stories that allow him to con others into giving him money.

Psychological addicts are particularly prone to lying. Compulsive gamblers are always in debt, and borrow from Peter to pay Paul. They tell lies to the bank manager to get loans for spurious projects, lie to their friends to help pay the bank, and so on.

Anorexics use all kinds of manipulative tricks to convince people that they are not starving themselves. They drink lots of water before weighing themselves, they hide the food they refuse to eat, they exercise excessively and take laxatives frequently in secret. Eventually lying becomes so ingrained the person may find it easier to lie than tell the truth and may begin to lie for no identifiable reason. For those who care for such people, it is extremely difficult. It is important to realize that the lies are not a personal betrayal, but rather a symptom of the addictive disorder.

Some people will steal whether they are addicted or not. They do so as a way of life and are recognized as thieves and criminals. Those who steal in order to feed an addiction don't fit this category. Most of us would rob our mother of her pension if we were deeply addicted and in need of a fix. Addictions require financial resources, especially drug addiction. If there are 1,000 heroin addicts in one city, who on average need $250 per day to feed their habit, this means that a very large sum of money will be spent on heroin in one week. This money has to be gained from some source or another, and most heroin addicts have very little money, so they must resort to dealing in drugs, or simply stealing money from friends, family, and acquaintances. This aspect of addiction leads to enormous levels of crime.

Other addictions also lead to financial problems. Every small town has its examples of people who drank away large inheritances and ended up destitute or gambled away successful businesses. Gamblers sometimes end up in jail for embezzlement. Telephone sex-lines have led some unfortunates to run up bills so large they end up remortgaging their houses.

People who cannot afford their addictions will find some way, legal or not, to get the money. Small wonder, then, that stealing is a feature of many addictions. In this sense, the adolescent who steals money for cigarettes is no different from the person who shoplifts to pay for heroin. The stealing is all part of addiction.

When someone is gradually being overtaken by addiction, his life goes out of control, and the regularity of life is lost. Late hours are kept, and he arrives home later and later in the small hours of the morning—perhaps he doesn't come home at all. Days are missed from work, and spurious excuses become less and less believable. Teenagers can miss school, or play truant, or be unable to get up in the morning as a direct result of toxic sedation of the body. The inability to function within a normal timetable may be a signal of advanced addiction. Work is often the last thing to go. It pays for the supply of alcohol or other substance and will be held on to for dear life. Most working addicts cannot afford to lose their jobs.

Every addiction has its particular effect on the body and mind. In the next chapter, there is a brief discussion of the more common types of drugs and their physical effects. Here we are interested in the general wear and tear associated with all addictions. The skin can lose its luster; spots and rashes become more common. The eyes seem sunken and dead, and this deathly appearance is exacerbated by weight loss or a bloated appearance.

The person can be fatigued all the time or he may be listless. He may appear nervous and agitated. His speech becomes monotonous and loses its animation. His gestures may slow down. He may appear to be functioning in a lower gear than is normal. He may become rundown, he often stops eating properly, and he may begin to show signs of physical deterioration. Personal hygiene can also be affected with less attention paid to physical appearance and cleanliness. These are common signs—but there are exceptions to every rule.

Because the addict's physical health is compromised, he becomes more prone to illness. Such illness is a secondary effect, meaning it is not caused directly by a particular substance. Infections cause respiratory problems. Aches and pains are diagnosed as flu or the common cold. Stomach problems are often seen as food allergies or gastroenteritis. Many of these mask the addiction that causes them. It is estimated that in the United States the treatment for illness caused indirectly by alcohol abuse alone runs to the sum of fifty billion dollars per year. And that is just one drug.

Other symptoms are directly related to the drug used. Flu-like symptoms can result from withdrawal effects. Digestive problems, including gastritis and pancreatitis, are particularly associated with alcohol abuse. Persistent coughing occurs for those people who smoke or snort their drugs. The list of possible physical illnesses is too long to present here. When illness seems to be recurring along with some of the other symptoms described above, one must consider the possibility that some chemical substance is being used.

# CHAPTER V

# Chemical Dependence

The mood-altering substances described here all have chemical components that affect brain functioning. It is important to explain briefly how the brain is affected by them.

It is more accurate to think of the brain not as one single unit, but as a combination of "mini-brains." At the top of the spinal chord where the nerve cells multiply and broaden out, we have the basic, simple brain that we share with primitive creatures, such as frogs and fish. This mini-brain controls the essential elements of staying alive—breathing, respiration, circulation, sensory experience, and automatic survival skills. It is the only part of the brain that is fully operational in a newborn infant.

Covering this simple structure is the limbic system which we share with more highly developed creatures, such as cats, dogs, and horses. This mini-brain controls physical movement and instinctual emotional responses. Powerful emotional reactions including rage, fear, and sexual desire are controlled by this part of the brain.

On top of this mini-brain is the most highly developed mini-brain, the cerebral cortex. This part provides human beings with the capacity to think, create, make choices, use language, and to experience very high levels of complex functioning. Very undeveloped at birth, the cerebral cortex continues to grow and develop throughout childhood.

A drug that primarily affects the limbic system will, for example, influence emotions, whereas one that affects the cerebral cortex will influence thought processes. Many drugs affect more than one part of the brain, and thus can have a generalized effect on thinking and feeling, as well as on basic bodily functioning.

The picture I have described above is simplistic—it does not reflect the incredibly complex nature of the brain. The vast network of connections between the different parts, and the almost infinite numbers of connections within each part, as well as the variety of brain functions, would take a complete book to describe. For the purposes of this guide, we ask simply where, on what part(s) of the brain, do drugs impact. And then we must ask how they do so. The answer to this second question lies in the way brain cells communicate with each other.

Every human feeling, thought, or action involves millions of nerve cells communicating with each other by using complex chemical messengers called neurotransmitters. Mood-altering drugs influence these neurotransmitters and thus influence the communication between brain cells. Different neurotransmitters are responsible for different areas and functions in the brain.

I will discuss various addictive chemicals in terms of the neurotransmitters that they are most likely to affect, thus explaining to some extent the results of taking these chemicals.

I am not suggesting that addiction is simply a physical problem. The previous chapter outlined some of the major psychological elements in addiction. I noted that in certain addictions these psychological forces are powerful enough to affect brain chemistry directly without the use of a chemical. Let us now turn to some of the most common addictive chemicals.

## ALCOHOL

Ethanol is a colorless, odorless, tasteless chemical that is the active ingredient in all alcoholic drinks. It is a byproduct of the chemical reaction involved in the fermentation of sugar and yeast. This active ingredient is a powerful depressant drug that retards or suppresses the functions of the brain and spinal chord, beginning with what are called the higher order functions, namely thinking, perception, control, etc. Lower order brain functions are those regulated by the deeper parts of the brain, and control bodily functions, including breathing and consciousness. The greater the level of alcohol consumed, the more widespread the suppression of brain activity.

A little alcohol makes most people more talkative, less inhibited, and often more elated. There is a more devil-may-care attitude, an ability to take some risks like chatting with someone you might otherwise feel shy with. Such effects occur because the normal inhibitions in everyday life are dismantled. These changes are at work in the recreational use of alcohol, and as such are often quite useful and enjoyable.

Larger amounts of alcohol further decrease control, leading to slurring of speech and lack of coordination. Social taboos and moral values are also diminished. This sometimes leads to inappropriate behavior, such as pinching someone's bottom in public. Control over the aggressive instinct also diminishes, leading, for example, to a fight with the partner insulted by the bottom pincher. With substantial levels of alcohol the drinker also begins to lose control of himself socially, morally, and physically. He has also lost his ability to judge just how much control he has lost. And he no longer is able to gauge how much total control he has given over to alcohol.

Let us take the familiar scenario of a wedding celebration where it is common for several people to get drunk, often in an inoffensive and playful manner. It is also common for people to be asked to sing. The drunken singer launches into a well-known ballad; intense passion is aroused within him, as he bellows out the song completely out of tune, He has no rhythm and he gets the words wrong. He has lost control as well as judgment. Those being inflicted with this experience (i.e., those who aren't sufficiently inebriated not to notice) may wonder how the singer could possibly not know how bad he sounds. The alcohol has destroyed the singer's realization of the situation. I bring this up to illustrate the profound effect of alcohol on a human being, his ability to evaluate his ability to function. He simply is not able to set right the situation.

Some people overestimate their capacity to drive safely and then may kill someone on the road. I recently heard a story about a heavy drinker who boasted that he used to drive home when he knew he was unable to walk. His judgment was so impaired he believed he could manage driving more effectively than walking!

Some statistics from the United Kingdom make clear the enormous impact inherent with alcohol. The *British Medical Journal* reports that alcohol is associated with 80 percent of deaths from fire, 65 percent of serious head injuries, 50 percent of murders, 40 percent of road traffic accidents, 30 percent of fatal accidents, 35 percent of marital breakdowns, and one in three incidents of child abuse. These statistics help clarify the point that any drug that diminishes control can also unleash many barbaric and destructive elements inherent in a human being. And, as more alcohol is consumed, the most primitive functions of the brain are eventually disabled, leading to coma and death.

There are, then, three broad levels of effect from the drug: a light disinhibiting effect, which functions as a social lubricant; a deeper level of disability, where control and judgment are impaired; and then gross disability, where alcohol poisoning leads to death.

People who become addicted to the drug ethanol are called alcoholics and are considered to be suffering from a condition called alcoholism. There are several reasons why these labels are widely used, and there is some argument for changing our way of understanding this problem. These issues are discussed in the section on recovery (see page 80). Here I will use these labels for the sake of clarity.

Alcoholism is a serious, life-threatening condition that not only destroys the fabric of an alcoholic's life, but also creates enormous problems for those close to him. This is particularly true for his spouse and children, whose lives are often indelibly marked by the effects of the long-term relationship with him.

The condition can be described as one whereby a person continues to drink alcohol, in spite of the obvious damage that it is doing to him, both physically and mentally. The condition has several features, which can best be described as three distinct stages: the adaptive (or early) stage; the dependent (or crucial) stage; and the deteriorative (or chronic) stage.

The adaptive stage of alcoholism is hard to differentiate from normal drinking, in terms of amounts and regularity. Many young people, for example, drink to excess as part of experimentation and rebellion and are not at this stage of alcoholism. The markers for this stage lie not so much in his drinking habits, but in the relationship he begins to have with drink.

Some characteristics are using alcohol to feel good, with a growing sense of loss or lack of enjoyment if it is unavailable; developing consistent patterns of drinking that are integrated into life patterns, while reducing activities where drink is absent; becoming defensive or argumentative if questioned about drinking (implying a growing defensive posture); and developing a tolerance for alcohol, i.e., needing to drink more and faster to get the desired effect.

The person associates mainly with other drinkers and chooses relationships with people who tolerate or actively encourage, drinking. These could be other problem drinkers, or those who are prepared to tolerate excess and unreliability. This stage for most people occurs in the late teenage years into early adulthood.

The dependent stage is characterized by a change from using drink to enhance mood or increase enjoyment, to using it to reduce anxiety and prevent withdrawal symptoms. At this stage it is used more directly as a drug fix, although the individual may not recognize this. The drinking increases, and the person begins to show signs of loss of control. He will now drink at times and in places that are inappropriate, such as early morning, during work, or at home alone. He will as well become very anxious about having his supply of alcohol available.

Personality changes being to occur. He cares less about other people and their opinion about him. His moodiness and preoccupation with self increase. He becomes less emotionally available, which generally leads to communication breakdown. Physical disorders may occur, including sleeplessness, nausea, and tremor. These are usually explained away, or used as a further excuse to drink (i.e., to calm the nerves). Deliberate attempts are made to hide the level of drinking, to explain it away, or to blame others. At this stage, the person is physically and psychologically dependent on alcohol. This stage can last between five and fifteen years.

The deteriorative stage is marked out by serious personality problems, which can include extreme mood swings, outbursts of rage, suicidal depression, and increasing isolation. Practical problems reach crisis proportions, financial difficulties emerge, problems at work may mean a threatened job loss. Personal relationships also founder, followed by complete breakdown in marriage and family relationships. Physical deterioration continues with digestive disorders, bloated appearance, liver damage (which can become terminal), loss of memory, and a host of other physical problems.

Sometimes the addict will talk about such problems to his doctor without any connection being made to the drinking problem that causes them. Up to 30 percent of hospital beds are taken up by people who are unrecognized alcoholics and not treated for their basic problem. Unless the person gets treatment that directly deals with his drinking, it is likely that death from disease, accident, or suicide will result.

An alcoholic could read the above description and use the information to convince himself and others that he didn't have a problem. Typically he would pick any symptom described above and say, "There, I told you I couldn't be an alcoholic. I don't suffer from sleeplessness, financial problems, mood swings, etc."

There are binge drinkers who break out once a month who are addicts; there are those who quietly drink themselves into a comatose state and do not argue or fight. No matter, the addiction is the failure to stop using alcohol, even when great damage is being done as a direct result of drinking. Sometimes the addict is the last person to see his addiction, and will continue in denial for as long as he can, sometimes ably assisted by those around him.

## NICOTINE

Nicotine is the active ingredient in tobacco, and is ingested by smoking or chewing (less popular now than in the past). Nicotine is a powerfully toxic stimulant. It is so toxic that two or three drops of pure nicotine injected into a horse will kill it. Nicotine increases the level of dopamine, a key neurotransmitter, in the emotional center (limbic system) of the brain, and thus affects mood. (A neurotransmitter is a naturally occurring chemical, produced by the body with the express purpose of helping the brain to function.)

Most people get their nicotine fix by smoking cigarettes and in doing so also ingest hundreds of other damaging chemicals, of which carbon monoxide and tar are the most toxic. These toxins add to the physical damage that occurs. All of the nicotine, 90 percent of the carbon monoxide, and 70 percent of the tar stay in the lungs during the smoking of a cigarette.

Most people start smoking during their teenage years, often as an attempt to cultivate an image of coolness, or rebelliousness. Despite all the warnings (or maybe because of them) few teenagers are truly aware of the dangers that they face in beginning to smoke. Until very recently, cigarette companies denied that cigarette smoking was addictive and harmful. Rather, they promoted their killer products with abandon. Advertising was predominantly concerned with image associations. Some brands were connected to the free spirit and the wide open frontier. Others suggested cool elegance. Still others connected their brand to affluence. Often in response to these suggestions and peer group pressure, people start smoking as teenagers and soon become addicts.

Nicotine is a stimulant that affects mood, decreases appetite, and can facilitate learning and memory. It is legal, widely promoted, and lethal. Studies in the United States show that cigarette smoking kills more people than the combined total of those who die from AIDS, cocaine, heroin, alcohol, fire, car accidents, murder, and suicide.

Cigarette smoking is perhaps the most dangerous and costly of all addictions. Its seduction lies in the fact that it does not cause immediate injury, but rather does devastating damage over a long period. The health bills facing the economy and the individual are enormous. Treatment for heart and lung diseases (caused by chronic low-level starvation of oxygen to all the major organs), as well as a host of cancers directly related to the toxic effects of nicotine and the other chemicals, soaks up huge financial resources. There is also the direct cost of sustaining the addiction. The average smoker will spend a great deal of money on cigarettes alone during his shortened life, money that could go a long way to provide far more life-enhancing activities. You might well ask, why do people do this to themselves? One answer lies in the nature of this form of addiction.

Any drug that is administered by smoking is more likely to impact quickly and intensely on the user. The speed at which it reaches the brain centers where it works makes it potentially more addictive. Nicotine also builds tolerance and creates withdrawal symptoms. There is a gradual increase in the number of cigarettes needed in order to satisfy the smoker's craving.

An interesting phenomenon in this regard occurs when a smoker absentmindedly lights a second cigarette before having finished the first one. Most people who smoke begin to experience withdrawal pangs within thirty minutes after finishing a cigarette. These withdrawal pangs increase in intensity if not satisfied, leading to the stereotypical coffee and cigarette first thing in the morning.

All of these are physical aspects of nicotine addiction, but psychological aspects also play an important role. The ease with which nicotine can be accessed and used and the plethora of situations that it is associated with it, make it psychologically more addictive. This combination of physical effect and psychological dependence make it extremely difficult to break the hold of nicotine. One study of polydrug users (those who use more than one type of drug) showed that nicotine was rated above heroin, methadone, amphetamine, barbiturates, LSD, marijuana, alcohol, and caffeine as the drug they could least do without. You only have to visit a convention of Alcoholics Anonymous to see hundreds of recovering alcohol addicts (many who have been to hell and back to gain sobriety) puffing away on the other very commonly used drug, nicotine.

## PRESCRIPTION AND OVER-THE-COUNTER DRUGS

Prescription drugs are those that are for the most part a useful and sometimes essential part of treatment for a variety of conditions. Morphine, for example, is a highly addictive pain-killing drug that plays an essential role in treating the pain associated with post-operative recovery, as well as terminal illness. Over-the-counter drugs (aspirin, for example) are those that are used to medicate certain conditions, but do not need a prescription and are therefore not controlled. In this section, I will examine only those prescription drugs that are most often associated with addiction and most open to abuse.

## MINOR TRANQUILIZERS

Of all prescription medication, the minor tranquilizers are most open to abuse and most likely to lead to addiction. This group of drugs is called minor in order to distinguish them from medication used for very serious, psychotic conditions. The label "minor" should not be interpreted to mean safe, or benign.

The most widely used tranquilizers are called benzodiazepines. In general, there are two forms: those that are used primarily to help ease the symptoms of anxiety and nervousness, and sleeping pills. In the former category, brands such as Valium, Librium, Xanax, and Ativan are some of the most common; in the latter, the names Mogodon, Halcion, Dalmane, and Royhypnol are well known. There are dozens of different brands on the market, all having the same basic effects.

These drugs act primarily on the central nervous system and in many ways mimic the effect of alcohol. More specifically, they increase the presence of a neurotransmitter called gamma-aminobutric acid, or GABA for short. This neurotransmitter is found in large quantities in various parts of the brain. It slows down the communication between brain cells. Thus, by increasing the presence of this neurotransmitter, tranquilizers slow down the individual's reactivity and experience, emotionally and intellectually.

Anxiety is a painful state of fearful vigilance, and any medication that slows down the system will also reduce these symptoms, leaving the individual more relaxed. Tranquilizers are, however, nonspecific, insofar as they do not simply act on anxiety—they slow down the whole system. Someone under the influence of tranquilizers may appear slightly drunk, slurring words, lacking in coordination, and generally unfocused. Another, less common, group of anti-anxiety medications is called beta-blockers. These drugs are used primarily for heart problems and sometimes for anxiety, because they act on the second-order symptoms of anxiety, namely heart rate and palpitations. These drugs are less addictive.

## TRANQUILIZER ADDICTION

Any medication or activity that reduces anxiety is potentially addictive. Anxiety is one of the most prevalent forms of mental suffering in the developed world, and most people are engaged—to a greater or lesser extent—in reducing, or avoiding it. Jogging, health clubs, television, counseling, eating, and a plethora of other activities are used by many people to this end. Tranquilizers are, however, particularly dangerous, because they build tolerance and create withdrawal symptoms.

Tolerance occurs with these drugs because the brain adapts to them and limits their impact, which means that the individual must take greater quantities in order to produce the same effect. And the withdrawal effects are particularly severe because they are used to avoid anxiety. When the drug is removed, the anxiety is still there, but there is now an additional problem. The activity level of the central nervous system increases when the drug is withdrawn, so the person is more sensitive to his fears and worries that still exist. Additionally, they now have to fear their fear, and wonder if they are going to go mad. For some people, addiction to tranquilizers is a nightmare.

Questions need to be asked about the use of chemicals to deal with anxiety, given that it seems to be such an endemic part of modern life. Anxiety is, in most cases, circumstantial and environmental and thus is not something that should be medicated. When the minor tranquilizers became widely available, they were immediately successful, and in some cases responsible for long-term, harrowing suffering by those who used them as a shortcut to emotional healing. The Rolling Stones' song "Mother's Little Helper" called attention to the widespread use of this type of medication among women in particular during the 1960s and 1970s. Because of the current awareness that these drugs are dangerous, they are now prescribed more cautiously, but a great deal of damage has been done.

There is also a serious danger of cross addiction with alcohol. It is very easy to see how a person who has used these prescription drugs for anxiety can move on to alcohol to escalate the sedating effects, or to replace the pills when the tranquilizers run out. This cocktail of tranquilizers and alcohol is a lethal mix and can lead to death from overdose.

Many years ago, I read a most vivid and illuminating story of the nature of tranquilizer addiction in the book, *I'm Dancing as Fast as I Can*. This true story shows the gradual takeover of the individual addicted to tranquilizers. In general, life becomes a journey marked out between pills. As worry and fearfulness make themselves felt, the individual takes a pill. Within a short period, there is a calming feeling of relaxation that gradually wears off, requiring another pill. Then there is the fear of the supply running out. The panic of finding oneself in a shopping center and realizing that the pills are at home leads to vertigo, dizziness, and shortness of breath, as the fear begins to rise like a wave. Night-time pills are needed to sleep, morning pills to help meet the day, lunch-time pills to help cope with the nervous feelings, tea-time pills to cope with coming home, or the spouse returning. On and on it goes, as the individual becomes completely lost in a fog of chemical sedation.

## AMPHETAMINES

Amphetamines are a group of drugs that were originally designed for medical purposes. They were synthesized after it was discovered that ephedrine was the active ingredient in an ancient Chinese herbal treatment for asthma. Amphetamine, the closest chemical equivalent to ephedrine, was very successful with asthma because it had a profound effect on the level of adrenaline in the body. Later, these drugs were used as appetite suppressants (slimming pills), and they were also used to treat mild depression. All of these effects were noted in the approval given by the American Food and Drug Administration (FDA) for their use as prescription medication.

Currently, amphetamines are not used widely for asthma—they are far more likely to be found on sale on the black market. They are often referred to as the poor man's cocaine (they have remarkably similar effects). A particularly dangerous and innovative form is that of the amphetamine derivative Methylamphetamine hydrochloride, with the name ice, or crystal meth, because of its transparent sheet-like crystals. It vaporizes easily and can be smoked, leading to a powerful high. A near relative to amphetamine is one of the active ingredients in the drug Ecstasy.

Amphetamine is now recognized as extremely addictive and dangerous. Consequently, its medical use is very restricted. It is mainly prescribed in the form of the drug Ritalin, used to treat the rather controversial condition called attention deficit disorder (ADD) in children. It is also used to treat the less common sleep disorder called narcolepsy.

Amphetamines gained prominence and infamy in the halcyon years of the drug culture, the 1960s. They were embraced and idealized by those who used them as a stand-alone fix that gave constant highs and extreme euphoria. This group of junkies was eventually given a name of its own within the drug culture—speed freaks. Others used the brands Benzedrine (bennies), Dexedrine, Quaaludes (ludes) to accentuate the altered states produced by LSD. The attraction of amphetamines to the drug-hungry subculture led to governmental concern and a crackdown on availability.

## AMPHETAMINE ADDICTION

Amphetamines are powerful stimulants that boost the activity of the neurotransmitters—dopamine, norepinephrine, and serotonin. They increase the level of activity in both the emotional and intellectual centers of the brain. Amphetamines were used regularly by the armed forces in both the Second World War and in Vietnam. They allowed people to go beyond normal endurance, both physically and mentally. Others, particularly university students, used them to help cram for exams. The heightened awareness and concentration levels produced by the drugs' effect on the cerebral cortex meant that people could study for nights without sleep, and still have the energy to arrive in time for the exam. Much disillusion followed, however, when they discovered that they could not recall what they had learned.

Amphetamines produce serious psychological addiction. They also increase the potential for massive emotional breakdown. One of the intriguing effects of heavy use is the phenomenon of amphetamine psychosis. This occurs when the individual shows the signs and symptoms of serious mental illness, namely schizophrenia. In most cases, the heavy user becomes increasingly paranoid and confused. Many murders have been committed by those in a full-blown, amphetamine-produced paranoia. This phenomenon was so widespread in the United States that it gave new meaning to the phrase, "speed kills."

Another major effect of heavy amphetamine use is what is termed "the crash," a state of complete exhaustion and emotional depression, occurring in the aftermath of the amphetamine high. There is a commonly accepted rule in psycho-pharmacology that "what goes up must come down." Many heavy users cannot bear the withdrawal effects and take opiates such as heroin, or tranquilizers, to ease the pain of the crash. This leads to cross addiction, and a very poor prognosis for a drug-free life.

## ANTIDEPRESSANTS

Prescribed antidepressants have some potential for addiction. It is commonly believed in the medical profession that these drugs are not addictive, a belief based on several assumptions. These drugs do not produce tolerance; that is, the user does not need to increase the dosage when taking them over a long period. Thus, they do not fulfill one of the important criteria for addiction. Secondly, in the initial stage they do not provide an immediate chemical effect that alters mood. Consequently, they are not attractive to an addictive drug user and have little sales value on the black market. The people who are addicted to antidepressants are likely to be under medical care and take their medication responsibly for "depressive illness." They will not, in general, know that they are addicted until they try to stop the medication. There are three different types of antidepressant medication: tricyclics, SSRIs (Selective Serotonin Reuptake Inhibitors) and MAOIs (Monoamine Oxidase Inhibitors). In terms of addictive potential, we are only interested in the first two because of the way they act on the brain.

MAOIs are more likely to be used when a person has not responded to either of the other types. MAOIs are prescribed cautiously, because they are extremely toxic, and if taken with certain foods or other medicine they can lead to massive cardiovascular crisis or stroke. Tricyclic antidepressants have a long history, and were originally developed for treatment of schizophrenia. They are now being replaced with a new-generation drug. the SSRIs, which boost the availability of the neurotransmitters norepinephrine and serotonin. For most of their history, it was considered that their impact on norepinephrine was most active in relieving depression. The SSRIs had side effects of nausea, dizziness, dry mouth, etc. The chemical effect of tricyclics was somewhat similar to that of amphetamines, but did not create the same experience in the user. This may be because amphetamines both increase the amount and also maintain the level of norepinephrine, whereas the tricyclics do not actually add to the levels.

As theories of depression developed, one line of inquiry suggested that these drugs were having their impact on depression by affecting the neurotransmitter serotonin and that perhaps a drug that acted on serotonin alone would be most effective. This research led to the new generation of SSRIs and the household name Prozac. Prozac and its near relatives, Seroxat and Lustrol, are now the most widely prescribed antidepressants, as well as becoming a cultural phenomenon in the United States. Many people who are not clinically depressed are taking these drugs to boost morale and energy levels. Like the amphetamine craze of the 1960s, we are seeing a medical treatment losing its clinical moorings and being brought into the consumer market simply to make people feel happier.

## ADDICTION TO ANTIDEPRESSANTS

We have seen above that these drugs do not produce tolerance and are therefore, strictly speaking, not addictive. They are, however, very potent, and users may become chemically dependent on them. Serotonin is one of the more important neurotransmitters related to mood. The part of the brain that is crucial to pleasure, appetite, and sleep regulation (the hypothalamus) is almost completely constructed of serotonin-based nerve cells. By increasing the availability of serotonin in this area of the brain, the user's mood, appetite, and sleep patterns are affected.

Serotonin also plays a more widespread role in other areas of the brain. Long-term use of antidepressants may lead to a compensation in the brain for the presence of greater levels of serotonin. The brain may react by lowering the production of serotonin, which can then cause painful withdrawal effects, and the person may experience deeper depression than before. This is often taken as proof that the medication is treating their depressive illness. There is, however, an alternative explanation.

By lowering the brain's sensitivity to serotonin, the very substance that is supposed to help people feel better makes them feel worse. It is my experience that some people getting off this kind of medication can experience harrowing emotional turmoil: mood swings, feeling overwhelmed, dizziness, and physical malaise all seem to be regular features of withdrawal. It is irresponsible for any practitioner to prescribe these drugs without informing the patient that he may find it difficult to stop taking them.

## THE OPIATES

This group of drugs is so named because they are derivatives of opium. The most common synthetic variations in medical usage are morphine, codeine, and methadone, used primarily as pain relievers. Sometimes after surgery, pain-relieving drugs are not strong enough. It is in these situations and with the terminally ill that morphine is used. Codeine is a milder opiate, but once it is swallowed, it is converted to morphine in the body. The powerfully addictive nature of these drugs has led to more cautious control on their distribution and usage. Until the turn of the century it was possible to buy morphine over the counter at the local apothecary.

Chemically, the opiates mimic the naturally occurring pain-relieving substances in the brain. These are called endorphins, and are involved in both pain relief and pleasure. Sexual intercourse and physical exercise lead to a release of endorphins that are experienced as feelings of pleasure. Injury may also lead to a release of endorphins, resulting in the relief of pain. Opiates share some similarities with tranquilizers, in their tendency to make the user feel drowsy and serene. However, they are most seductive because they produce a tremendous rush of warm well-being. It is this effect that has led to their voluntary usage.

I will discuss addiction to opiates in the section on illegal drugs, because heroin is the primary opiate of abuse and yet shares most of the characteristics of those drugs used in conventional medicine.

## ILLEGAL DRUGS

Thus far we have discussed the addictions that cause the greatest damage to human beings. It should be noted that the negative impact on society and on human life from the use of illegal drugs is miniscule in comparison to the damage from those that are legal. When a young person dies after taking one Ecstasy tablet, there is a major hue and cry in the media. However, this one death is far outmatched by several hundred people dying daily from alcohol- or nicotine-related illness. When was the last time a newspaper gave headline attention to an ordinary person dying from liver failure due to alcohol abuse or from emphysema due to cigarette smoking?

A great deal of the damage associated with the use of illegal substances is a direct result of the fact that their usage has been criminalized. Let us take a simple example. Heroin is a very powerful drug, and violence is associated with its use. People are attacked by strung-out addicts who are desperate for money to buy a fix. Gangland drug lords kill each other or anyone who gets in their way for access to the incredibly profitable black market.

These effects have nothing to do with the actual effect of heroin on the addict. Heroin does not make people violent. In fact it's quite the opposite: it induces drowsiness, apathy, and euphoria. The drug that is most likely to lead to violence in its direct chemical effect is—you guessed it—alcohol.

This point is important in any rational discussion about illegal drugs. We must try to separate the effects of the drug itself on the individual from the effects on society and the individual when he has to become a criminal in order to gain access to the drug. These are two different issues. Our concern is with the first. The second belongs to the legal and political strategies to control the availability of these drugs, and is beyond the scope of this book.

## HALLUCINOGENIC DRUGS

These drugs affect people's perception of reality, and they are specifically used for this purpose. While some of the drugs discussed earlier have hallucinatory effects, none are prescribed or used for this reason. Hallucinogenic drugs disinhibit the control of the normal waking mind and lead the user to a different state of consciousness, with a heightened sensory awareness of color, light, and the senses.

William James, the psychologist, describes the effect of these drugs.

> One conclusion was forced on my mind, and my impression of its truth has ever since remained unshaken. It is that our normal waking consciousness, as we call it, is but one special type of consciousness, whilst all about it, parted from it by the flimsiest of screens, there lie potential forms of consciousness entirely different. We may go through life without suspecting their existence, but apply the requisite stimulus, and at a touch they are there in all their completeness….No account of the universe in its totality can be final which leaves these other forms of consciousness quite disregarded.

Since William James's time, and particularly during the experimental years of the 1960s, the use of hallucinogens has become widespread.

The specific effect of hallucinogens on the chemistry of the brain remains a mystery. They seem to selectively reduce the impact of external stimuli by blocking certain neurotransmitters, while increasing the brain's sensitivity to internal and often subconscious data. In a way, it is inaccurate to call these drugs hallucinogens because they do not create any new information or mental events. Rather, they increase the user's attention to and focus on experiences that already exist. Recent research suggests that the active ingredient in much of the chemical effects is a naturally occurring brain substance called trypta-mine, which is released by the pineal gland.

A more recent argument is that while they do not produce new mental events, neither do they rely totally on internal sensations. Instead they attune the mind to become accessible to a different reality, one that is just as important and "real" as the events noticed in ordinary levels of consciousness. Thus, many of the events that occur under the influence of hallucinogenic drugs belong to the spiritual and esoteric plane of human consciousness.

An interesting analogy may clarify this viewpoint. Compare the human brain to a radio receiver and consider the way the brain may be receptive to certain kinds of signals. Tuning a radio to a certain frequency allows us to access certain channels and equally denies us access to others. Perhaps different forms of consciousness are like the tuner on a radio—they may open the mind to voices and signals of a certain reality, while closing accessibility to others. In normal waking consciousness, our brains are tuned to the channel of what can experienced through the senses and processed by the intellectual program that exists in our minds as a result of learning. It is argued by many that this area of experience is only one of a number of different realities that can be experienced, each requiring a different form of consciousness.

Everybody experiences the obviously different forms of consciousness involved in dreaming while asleep on one hand and waking on the other. Perhaps there are other forms of consciousness, ones that can be encountered through various types of meditation, ritual practices, and drugs. Much of the evidence coming from a variety of cultures, as well as from certain areas of psychotherapy, suggest that this is the case. The question remains whether the voices, visions, and messages delivered to the individual in altered states of consciousness have an objective, though secret reality, or whether they are simply the product of overactive imaginations stimulated by the juices of the brain. It is beyond the scope of this book to examine this fundamentally important question.

## ADDICTION TO HALLUCINOGENS

The more common hallucinogens are marijuana, LSD, DMT, mescaline, psilocybin (either synthetic or in the form of magic mushrooms), and some forms of MDMA (Ecstasy), There is little evidence that these drugs are physically addictive.

Although marijuana is in a class of its own, I have included it here because it is mildly hallucinogenic. It is by far the most commonly used illegal substance, smoked as hashish or grass as a recreational drug by hundreds of millions worldwide. Evidence suggests that it is less toxic than cigarette smoke or alcohol. Thus, there is much argument in favor of decriminalization.

Marijuana is psychologically addictive. It is an attractive drug, assisting people to tune out of reality, escape the pressures of life, and reach a serene experience. Most people seem to be able to use it now and then with little or no long-term impact or side effects. Others, however, become consistently stoned, apathetic, lacking in concentration, and somewhat paranoid. It is my experience that this level of use can ruin a person's life.

LSD, DMT, and mescaline are far more powerful hallucinogens than marijuana. They are the synthetic equivalents of natural hallucinogenic substances found in a variety of plants and fungi, including the desert root-plant, peyote, and the vine banisteriopsis. These plants and others like them have been used for centuries in the rituals of many cultures, including that of

Native Americans. They are usually considered sacred and are used carefully within the cultural taboos of the tribe or group. The synthetic equivalents are, however, not given the same respect, nor do they have the same purpose. They, like marijuana, are not physically addictive. They do, however, build tolerance and cross tolerance. This means if the drug of choice is LSD, the individual will have to use more and more to get an effect, and he will have to use larger amounts of the other hallucinogens, such as mescaline, if he changes over to them.

LSD, DMT, and mescaline are psychologically addictive and, in my opinion, extremely dangerous. I do not mean that they have no value. Their history within certain cultures and the interest that is taken in them as therapeutic agents in a clinical setting suggest that they may have some value for emotional healing and spiritual growth. In the vast majority of cases, these drugs are used to tune out of conscious reality and to provide an electrifying sensory overload, which the user hopes will be positive and enjoyable.

Crucial to the use of these drugs are two important considerations, namely the environment in which the drugs are taken and the mindset of the user. Most people who use these drugs do not understand the importance of these factors and are playing Russian roulette with their psychological integrity. For those who have a fragile identity within their psychological makeup and who try to journey beyond the gray zone of their lives by using these drugs, insanity is a real risk. Stable, mature persons have less to fear. Then again, do we know ourselves well enough? Do we really know the demons that lurk in our unconscious to tempt them with such elixirs, into conscious awareness and experience?

## THE OPIATES

We have examined the basic effects of opiate drugs in the discussion of prescription drugs above. Here we are mainly concerned with heroin. There is a certain irony in the name which comes from the word "hero"—it was expected that heroin would be heroic in helping addicts free themselves from heroin's close relatives, morphine and opium. The cure proved worse than the disease: heroin turned out to be far more potent and addictive than the drugs it was to replace. Moreover, its use led to many other problems. Heroin addicts face huge risks from contaminated needles, as well as the toxic side effects from contaminated street heroin.

Other opiates are morphine, methadone, pethedine, and codeine. Certain compounds have been synthesized from these prescription painkillers, the best known being China white, a synthetic version of heroin that is many times stronger than morphine.

## OPIATE ADDICTION

Opiates are physically and psychologically addictive. Like alcohol, there are recognizable stages in its progression, no matter whether the addict is a doctor or pharmacist addicted to pethedine or an unemployed junkie. During the adaptive stage, the opiate is used to cope with stress or emotional pain, or to produce a high. This will lead to tolerance, so that greater amounts are needed, and withdrawal symptoms occur when the drug's effects wear off.

The move to the next stage, dependency, occurs much faster with opiates than with alcohol. Usually within weeks, the person becomes physically and emotionally dependent on the drug. This stage is marked by strong craving for the drug, more intense withdrawal effects, and more difficulty getting high. The focus now becomes a desperate attempt to ward off the intensely painful withdrawal symptoms. Additionally, the drug becomes the center of attention, and the addict is obsessed with its availability. Criminal activity increases if there is no ready access to the drug, particularly if the drug is illegal. Sexual performance deteriorates, and other physical problems begin to occur, particularly for those using contaminated needles or street heroin that has been cut with impure substances.

The chronic stage leads to a complete collapse of moral, intellectual, and emotional functioning, with the attendant loss of family, financial ruin, deep depression, and a strong risk of suicide or death by overdose. Without help at this stage, the person will die or end up in jail as a direct or indirect result of his addiction.

## PSYCHOSTIMULANTS

This group includes the amphetamines discussed above. They differ from the opiates and hallucinogens in that their primary function is to increase the activity level of the central nervous system. Their effect is to heighten energy, speed up reactions, and give a boost to all the senses. The most common illegal stimulants are cocaine, its synthetic equivalent, crack, and MDMA, better known as Ecstasy, originally developed in Germany in 1914 as an appetite suppressant. It is a potent combination of hallucinogenic and amphetamine chemicals, and is the drug of choice of the rave generation of the 1990s. When combined with rave music, it induces an altered state of consciousness, marked by a massive increase in energy (the amphetamine effect), euphoric feelings of connection to others, and oceanic bliss (why it is termed the love drug). After using the drug, people have died from dehydration, heart failure, and chemical collapse. These dangers are, however, the extreme end of the spectrum, and users tend to dismiss any warnings as propaganda by conservatives in society. The drug *is*, however, extremely dangerous because of its come-down effects and its long-term impact on the chemistry of the brain. Its effect on serotonin levels can lead consistent users into long-term depression. It also leads some users into cross addiction with heroin or other opiates that are used to cope with the crash—the emotional fatigue and burnout experienced in the aftermath of the high.

Cocaine is a powerful stimulant that affects the central nervous system by increasing the levels of dopamine, serotonin, and norepinephrine. It has been used for thousands of years by Indians in South America to combat fatigue and hunger. It was ingested by chewing coca leaves, which meant a much slower intake and less of a high. It was introduced into Europe in the 1850s as a local anaesthetic. Sigmund Freud prescribed it to a friend as a cure for his morphine addiction, thus creating the first known cocaine addict. Freud himself then became addicted to cocaine.

It is used in medicine today in the form of the Brompton Cocktail, a combination of cocaine and other painkillers, to alleviate the suffering of terminally ill cancer patients. Crack is a form of cocaine. Since it is smoked, it gives a faster, more intense hit. Crack is particularly dangerous—it leads to more deaths from heart attacks, strokes, and damage to the heart and lungs, than snorting cocaine powder.

## COCAINE ADDICTION

As the body metabolizes or breaks down cocaine, there does

not appear to be any illness or physical pain caused by the drug's absence. Thus, cocaine is not considered to be addictive. However, cocaine use does produce a strong craving and loss of well-being in some people. It may be that these cravings are in fact physical rather than psychological in origin.

We have more evidence that consistent use of cocaine has a devastating effect on the brain's reactivity to dopamine, one of the key neurotransmitters. It would appear that by damaging the brain's receptivity to dopamine, the user runs the risk of long-term, chronic depression that is physical in origin and can be considered a delayed withdrawal reaction.

Cocaine addiction tends to progress through three stages, with the experimental stage first, where cocaine is used out of curiosity and to enhance feelings. There is no major impact on social, emotional, or physical functioning. Generally, the person uses the drugs only when cocaine is offered to him and only socially, in the company of other people.

This first stage can lead rather quickly to the second, compulsive stage, where there is a gradual disruption of lifestyle. The addict buys cocaine more regularly, begins to distance himself from non-users, and at the same time tries to change. He begins to experience mood swings with increased social withdrawal and financial troubles caused by his overspending.

The third stage is marked by his growing inability to function in relationships and work. He has difficulty sleeping and eating. Very high doses are used, leading to serious medical problems. He may try other drugs in order to cope with the growing disorder in his life, the terrible depressions, and the emotional crashes when he is coming down from the fix. He is totally preoccupied with the drug, which is now used to feel normal and to cope with guilt. In order to support his habit, he may become a dealer, thief, or embezzler. There is a growing risk of serious physical damage to his heart, lungs, and nasal cavity.

## MISCELLANEOUS ADDICTIVE SUBSTANCES

Thus far, we have discussed the more commonly used addictive drugs. There is a growing market for all kinds of chemically prepared, mood-altering substances and new potions or combinations are continually being brought into the drug-hungry market. A recent addition is Ketamine (called special K). This was widely used in Vietnam as a battlefield anaesthetic. It is hallucinogenic and produces an extreme relaxed state. Side effects can lead to paralysis and long-term medical problems. Another is GHB, sometimes known as liquid Ecstasy. It has the same effects and side effects as Ketamine. Amyl nitrate (poppers), used to increase the intensity of sexual orgasm, particularly in the gay community, is now part of the nightclub scene.

Solvents that are inhaled are particularly dangerous. These include antifreeze, paint thinner, correction fluid, and glues. Most contain an industrial solvent called Tuolene, which may be the active ingredient. The main effect is a dizzy high. These can cause serious harm to the lungs and throat, and severe, irreparable brain damage.

Another highly addictive drug is caffeine, which is a stimulant, and leads to quite severe withdrawal symptoms for some people who try to cut down on its use.

# CHAPTER VI

# Psychological Addiction

Is it valid to describe activities as addiction that do not involve an addictive substance? Some argue that the meaning of addiction is lost if it is used to refer to activities other than drug-taking. I have some sympathy with this viewpoint, but it is becoming clear that we cannot distinguish the biology of addiction from its psychological elements. All addiction involves changing the chemistry of the brain. Drug abuse does it in a more intense and recognizable manner. Recent research shows, however, that certain behaviors also impact on brain function. These are therefore addictive even within the biological sense of the word.

It seems more useful to speak of two broad areas of addiction: those that relate to certain chemicals, i.e., chemical addiction, and those that relate to activities, i.e., addictive behaviors. This chapter concerns some of the major psychological addictions.

## COMPULSIVE GAMBLING

For many people, the notion that someone can become addicted to gambling seems rather strange. That a person can feel a powerful compulsion to bet on a horse or spend hours in front of a slot machine seems ridiculous, so easy to avoid.

However, addiction to gambling is much more complex than simply wanting desperately to take a chance. The obvious damage that is incurred financially is often accompanied by the equal emotional, spiritual, and intellectual destruction. The intricate nature of gambling addiction is not understood because it has only in recent years been recognized as a serious disorder.

Gambling addicts tend to deal with emotional distress by using defense mechanisms of distraction and rationalization. In other words, like other types of addicts, they have a lot of problems coping with their feelings. What tends to set these addicts apart is their use of thinking as a means of avoidance. Once this pattern is established, they are prime candidates for gambling problems. Having tasted the experience of gambling, they have found a situation that can utilize all their mental energy. The risks inherent in betting occupy their minds, and eventually take it over completely. Allied to this is the adrenaline surge that is inherent in the excitement of the risk of winning or losing.

Compulsive gamblers will bet on anything or, more accurately, will try to turn everything into an opportunity to gamble. A recent experience will illustrate this point. On a visit to London, I was taking a guided tour that included some of the clubs associated with the English aristocracy. One of the bits of information offered by the guide was an account of a member of the royal family who bet a vast sum of money on which of two raindrops trickling down the window pane would reach the bottom first. Most gamblers do not indulge in such trivial stuff, but the principle behind their activities is the same. Gradually, a cycle of obsessional thinking about gambling takes a firmer and firmer hold on the person's mind. Fatigue and financial loss lead to taking higher and more impulsive betting risks, with even less chance of success. Emotionally exhausted from the outcome of this addiction, the gambler has fewer and fewer resources to use in his relationships, his family, and his work. Gradually, as financial problems mount, he becomes more and more secretive and deceitful, mortgaging more and more of his resources, losing more and more money, all the while hoping for the big win that will relieve him of this burden. Should this win occur, he is likely to lose it all again, and so the cycle continues. This is akin to someone trying to dig themselves out of a hole using a shovel—all they do is get in deeper.

Most untreated gambling addicts eventually lose everything they own—and often a lot of what they don't own—leading to lifelong debt and financial impoverishment.

Emotional withdrawal follows and deeper anxiety sometimes leading to suicide. Sometimes the addict turns to some other addictive substance such as alcohol. Over a period of years, the person becomes an emotional and spiritual wreck.

## EATING DISORDERS

Perhaps the best example of addictive behavior is found among those who suffer from eating disorders. In the main, there are three different types of disorder: compulsive overeating, bulimia, and anorexia nervosa. Overeating is the least complex of these disorders. For the most part, the individual craves food and eats beyond the body's natural requirements, leading to obesity and a variety of physical disorders, usually resulting in early death. Food is primarily used as a mood-altering substance—a drug rather than a nutritional requirement. This is the key to understand this as an addiction.

Furthermore, certain types of food, particularly white sugar, refined flour, and chocolate, lend themselves to use as drugs. White sugar gives an instant boost to the energy system, followed by low blood sugar fatigue. The average American consumes forty to forty-five teaspoons of sugar per day. White flour is a dead food that is usually combined with sugar and a host of food additives, all having chemical effects. Chocolate contains phenylalanine, a substance related to mood that is found in small quantities in the brain, as well as theobromine, which has a stimulant effect. These are the most common forms of what are known as trigger foods, foods that, when taken, lead one to bingeing. It is likely that strong effects on the brain chemistry are triggered by the psychological association with the taste and texture, as well as the direct impact on body chemistry.

Evidence suggests that overeating is in some cases a result of food allergy; new methods of blood analysis are showing encouraging results in tracking down food sensitivities for some overeaters. The roots of most overeating problems are, however, emotional in origin. We now know that early life experiences have a profound effect on the way that the brain constructs itself, and furthermore that the associations between emotional states and certain experiences are deeply ingrained in the brain pathways.

It is also true to say that one of the earliest associations in infancy is the connection between being fed and the feeling of comfort and safety. For some people, this association appears to continue for complex reasons into adult life; this leads them to associate, often unconsciously, the experience of eating with emotional happiness. Because eating does not in fact heal emotional pain or solve emotional problems, an individual can find himself in a continual cycle of overeating—relief, emotional distress, further eating, relief, emotional distress, and so on.

This cycle is indistinguishable from those involved in other drug addictions.

Bulimia is often considered to be an attempt by overeaters to minimize the physical effect of their disorder by preventing the intake of calories. This disorder is the cycle of bingeing on food and then purging the body by vomiting and using laxatives, along with excessive exercise. This cycle is extremely damaging to the digestive system, can damage the heart, deplete essential potassium levels, rot the teeth, and affect skin and hair. It is likely that bulimia has stronger links to anorexia nervosa than it has to overeating.

Anorexia nervosa, originally called the slimmers' disease, is dangerous, addictive behavior that involves compulsive starvation and obsession with body weight and image. It is fatal in up to 20 percent of cases. Few disorders reflect the power of the mind as this one. At some stage, the person—very often an adolescent girl—begins to focus on body image and starts to control food. This is, of course, a very common behavior among adolescents who wish to remain slim, who have adopted the notion that being slim is a necessary part of being attractive.

A certain number of these young people find that within a short time their desire to control food has turned into a compulsion, and a nightmare. Losing more and more weight, their perception begins to change and they lose any accurate view of their own bodies. They see fat where there is none, they can look at their emaciated figures in a mirror and see a fat person looking back.

Parents and friends of the anorexic individual begin to panic and try all kinds of pressure to get the person to eat. This generally leads the individual to become manipulative and clever in disguising their starvation. Telling lies, acting out, and a plethora of other types of devious behavior are symptoms of the disorder, rather than any character flaw in the individual.

In many cases, bulimia seems to occur as a symptom of anorexia. Because anorexia is centrally a compulsion to control what is a primal biological imperative, namely eating, a tremendous conflict emerges between the intense reaction of the body to starvation, and the almost religious zeal to prevent food being taken. As the conflict heightens, the craving for food gets stronger; if the individual capitulates—especially with a trigger food, such as a cake, or chocolate bar—a massively overwhelming compulsion may ensue, where the individual eats to the point of exhaustion.

The terror then builds because the starving body is satisfied and the obsessive mind screams to get rid of the food. Vomiting, panic-stricken exercise, and laxatives are attempts to flush the body. Eventually, some semblance of peace ensues as control is regained. The body has been further damaged, and the cycle begins to build again. Eventually, the persons either recover in their own time, or get the help they need to recover; others starve to death.

There is little evidence to suggest that anorexia or bulimia is a biochemical disorder. It is more likely that any biological features are symptoms rather than causes of this syndrome. The vast majority of people who become anorexic are adolescent girls. The incidence rate has increased dramatically in the last two decades, and existing statistics suggest that 1 percent of Europeans and Americans will encounter this problem. Recent studies confirm that Argentina is fast becoming the anorexic capital of the world, with a rate four times that of the United States. These statistics are strong evidence that there are major cultural influences in the development of this disorder. As with most addictions, the social climate and the values and taboos of different societies influence the kinds of addiction that become prevalent.

## SHOPPING

The idea that culture affects the prevalence of certain types of addiction is further supported by the advent of compulsive shopping as an addictive disorder. A recent bumper sticker sums it up nicely, "Born to Shop." In societies where basic physical needs are met, and profit making is the central function of business, a whole superstructure is created to encourage and beguile people into buying what they don't really need. This structure includes convincing people that owning certain goods meets psychological needs, such as status, power, attraction to the opposite sex, security, and so on.

Most people in modern society are to some extent prey to the illusions wrought upon them through marketing strategies, and most get some comfort and pleasure from accumulating possessions in this manner. For some, however, the experience of shopping becomes compulsive and addictive. In general, as with most addictions, the activity is carried on in order to meet needs that it cannot meet, and is often driven by unconscious motives and emotions.

People who shop addictively tend to obsess on the shopping trip, distracting themselves from difficulties or problems by focusing on the pleasurable feeling they get when they visit the shops. The focus is not on whether the items are needed or even desired. The focus is on the act of buying, and it is this act that is central to the disorder. This explains why some addicts buy several pairs of the same shoes or the same clothes, knowing that they will not use them. The need to buy is the driving force—it doesn't really matter what is bought.

Closer examination reveals that underlying forces are at work. The person may be seeking to replace an emptiness within, or feels somehow more powerful by virtue of a buying spree. All the attendant experiences of the shopping expedition may also have a subconscious impact. The feeling of being anonymous in the crowd, or a sense of belonging, or simply the sense of attention being paid by the shop assistant may all be at work. Psychological addiction to shopping is as individual as the addict. Long-term recovery, as with most addictions, involves understanding the meaning of the addiction for each individual and the forces that are particularly at work in each situation.

## THE SILVER SCREEN

Addiction to television is as old as the apparatus itself. It is marked by a compulsive need to tune out of everyday reality and to enter the world of the soap opera, constant replays of the news, and channel surfing. Like most useful and beneficial things, television can become a source of great loss and waste. Television addicts lose the ability to be alone, or perhaps more accurately, may never have developed a mature sense of their own identity, as well as a motivation to learn and grow. Perhaps life is just too difficult, and it is easier to live an existence in the unreal world produced by the media moguls.

We have seen in the discussion of drug addiction that two key elements are tolerance and withdrawal: tolerance meaning a need for more of the substance to get relief or a high, and withdrawal meaning the growth of insecure, anxious, and painful feelings when the substance is not available. Television addicts spend more and more of their waking hours locked into television. They feel odd and uncomfortable in the silence when it is turned off.

The growth of this kind of addiction has seen increasing magazine publications devoted to the story lines of soaps. A person can now read about the transplant that Bill is waiting for and wonder if it will succeed, and if his wife will find out that he has been having an affair with Glenda when she visits him at the hospital. Coffee breaks at work may be spent discussing this issue, all in an amazing acceptance that fictional characters created by scriptwriters have taken on a greater reality in the mind of the addict. Recently one daily newspaper carried front-page pictures of two people crying in each other's arms. This was the reported break-up of the relationship between these two soap opera characters—it had no bearing on any reality.

Television provides entertainment, recreation, and education. It is perhaps one of the great additions to quality of life for many people. It is, however, potentially dangerous for some who become addicted to it as means of avoiding any constructive approach to living with themselves and others.

The advent of computer technology has brought a new level of expression to this addiction. The introduction of computer games to children and the Internet to adults provides a more fertile and perhaps insidious form of television addiction. A recent report described a mother whose children were taken into foster care. They were found unkempt, hungry, and crying, smeared with their own feces, while she plugged away for twelve to fourteen hours a day on the World Wide Web.

Children whose intellect and brain functions are still being formed are particularly vulnerable to computer game addiction.

The rise of attention deficit problems among school-age children may be directly related to exposure to computer games. More insidiously, lack of control over the level of exposure to these games may blunt the development of creativity and social skills, leaving them more prone to other kinds of addiction in later life.

## SEX ADDICTION

Even more recent is the discovery that people can become addicted to sexual experiences. It may be that sexual addiction is a relatively new phenomenon, or that it has always existed and is only now coming to light. My view on the matter is that addictions in general are culture bound. This means that people tend to become addicted to substances and activities that have some cultural license. Thus, for example, the Japanese are more likely to become addicted to amphetamines, the Chinese to opiates, and the Irish to alcohol. The sexual revolution in the 1960s and 1970s has now established itself as a more liberal and permissive view of sexual behavior. Casual sex is now a social reality in most Western societies, allowing a greater scope for addiction to develop.

Like most addictions, sexual addiction has certain defining characteristics. Sex addicts are compulsively engaged in the use of sexual experience for emotional distraction and relief. Their sexual behavior has little or nothing to do with intimacy or relationship. Nor has it anything to do with the relatively normal sexual needs that some people express by having a number of sexual partners, particularly during their early adulthood. Rather, sex addiction is a compulsively driven need to use sex to relieve the addict's sense of inner emptiness, or to alleviate feelings of anxiety or distress.

Modern society offers the sex addict an almost inexhaustible supply of sex-related stimulation. Sex toys, pornography, and sex guides can all be used to intensify sexual excitement and relief. By tuning out reality by consistently using fantasy and masturbation, the sex addict gradually erodes any semblance of normal sexuality (which for most includes a certain level of fantasy and masturbation). Eventually, the ability to experience true sexual love and intimacy is corrupted. Sex addicts confuse the biochemical sensations of sexual stimulation for the spiritual connection involved in sexual love. As the feelings of emptiness increase, the person tries harder to fill it with what is actually causing the emptiness, leading to the futile cycle that seems to be a central element in all addiction, namely, using something to meet one's needs that can't really meet those needs, and that damages the person in the process.

## ADDICTION TO WORK

Perhaps the most socially condoned and approved addiction is related to work. It is a very common disorder, which on the outside appears rather normal, but its effects are very destructive to any healthy, balanced life. Workaholics are people whose existence becomes completely dominated by work. Many of the elements of other addictions described above play a part also in work addiction and do not need to be repeated here. One aspect, however, that appears to be specific to this form of addiction is the need to secure the future through the accumulation of wealth or assets. Workaholics are generally fearful of financial ruin, and through their great need to accumulate may take major financial risks and end up in financial trouble.

Insecurity is a strong element in work addiction. Those close to the addict experience the loss of day by day security in the relationship, as the addict tries to make the future secure for his family. Many workaholics have come from backgrounds where there was financial worry, sometimes as a result of parental addiction to alcohol. In their effort never to experience it again, they end up ruining their health and happiness through overwork.

Another strong element in workaholism is pride. Having experienced conditional love as a child, many addicts believe that their worth is based on their success and in the amount of money they make. Even as the wealth accumulates, the work addict cannot enjoy its benefits. Deeply unhappy within himself, his money cannot buy peace of mind, love, or fulfillment. Each job well done and each substantial financial gain only give a fleeting feeling of satisfaction that must be repeated again and again. A stranger to his partner and children, the work addict strives harder and harder to find that elusive feeling of being a worthwhile human being.

Gradually the years roll on, and the person finds himself more and more frustrated. Perhaps he experiences a traumatic mid-life crisis, underpinned by the recognition of his reduced energy and his recognition of being overtaken by men younger than himself. In this case, the individual is prey to other forms of addiction, to sexual acting out or major depression. The degrees to which these storms are weathered are a good indication whether some form of physical or mental crisis will eventually overtake the person, leading to early death, suicide, or emotional breakdown.

## RELIGIOSITY

One message emerges from the above that most psychological addictions are a distortion of otherwise beneficial, healthy aspects of human life. Most good things can be used addictively—this also holds true of religion. In general, the religious ethos of a culture is regarded as the guardian of its moral values and ethics. Religion can, however, become a force for great destruction. Religious addiction has little to do with the great teaching of most religions. Rather, it is the use of religion as a method of rigid self-control, the suppression of life, a vehicle for prejudice, and the harbinger of self-destructive guilt and shame. This form of religiosity has nothing to do with true spirituality, nor the belief systems that promote love, value, and respect.

Religious addiction can be seen in people in each major denomination. It has a different flavor, depending on whether it is rooted in a Judeo-Christian or Islamic bent on the one hand, or the more esoteric and mystical focus of the East on the other. In the former, there is more likely to be a denial of feelings; a belief that authority is more important than relationship; a rigorous application of doctrinal law with no reference to its relevance to a particular situation; and an alienation from all people who do not share the worldview of the group. In the latter, the emphasis is on losing the person's ability to think and giving up a sense of identity. Constant focus on tuning out of current difficulties leads to an inability to function, and a disconnection from others.

Religious addicts are, in general, idealistic, emotionally vulnerable people who fall prey to the promise of a particular group or system. They end up trying to contain their unhappiness and insecurity by wrapping it up in the certainties of their religious belief system, at the same time depending on the group members and leader for affirmation and emotional nurturing. This combination does not work because, on the one hand, reality has a way of insisting on being heard and, on the other, the group members are unable to give healthy nurturing because they are fragmented themselves.

Deeper dissatisfaction and distress are interpreted as not worshipping properly, or not being attentive to the rules, or not meditating properly. Such criticism leads to greater efforts and more soul searching. Anguish continues until the individual becomes a constricted, emotionally frozen tape recorder, or gets the courage to leave the group. It is likely that on leaving he will adopt some other addiction unless help is received. When this happens, it reinforces the other group members' belief that the world out there is evil, and that they should work hard at staying within the numbing embrace of their religious ideology.

## ADDICTIVE RELATIONSHIPS

The notion that people can become psychologically addicted to another human being is recent. This is a complex and epidemic problem. In general, an addictive relationship is one in which a person consistently tries to change another person in order to get their own needs met. Or it is a relationship in which a person is consistently hurt by their partner emotionally and sometimes physically. Or it is a relationship in which a person is unable either to change their patterns or leave the relationship.

People who are addictively involved with another person tend to have low self-esteem, a high tolerance for suffering, a need to define their worth in terms of other people's opinions, an overestimation of the suffering of others, an underestimation of others' ability to help themselves, and a sense of failure when they cannot make their partner happy. In essence, they are unable to relate to themselves and to others, a severe form of dysfunction. In general, an addictive relationship is a mind-numbing, emotionally crippling, life-threatening condition.

Low self-esteem is the beginning of relationship addiction. This is usually the legacy of a difficult childhood, when the child is unsupported, unloved, and given little affection, admiration, praise, or guidance. Some children will, as a result of these deficiencies, become completely dependent on the valuation of others in order to feel good about themselves. The periods of childhood and adolescence have, as their purpose, the formation of people whose sense of identity is intact, who have a high level of love and respect for themselves. Without these positive formative influences, people can wander through life desperately searching for others to give them that sense of self-esteem. As a result, such persons become hostages to anyone who gives them praise or affection.

A person in an addictive relationship accepts the unacceptable. Having learned not to expect a lot from others, he is surprised when someone has a positive attitude towards him. The addictive person may marry the first person who shows any real interest on that basis alone and is consequently left struggling for years in a relationship that from the outset did not have what he needed, or even wanted. A high tolerance for suffering and the capacity for endurance often lead to a life of unhappiness and stress. Fear plays a significant part in addictive relationships. The stakes are very high—the need for love and acceptance are intense, but are bounded by an equally intense fear of rejection.

People in addictive relationships do not have a secure sense of their own identity. They look outside themselves to gauge their worth. It is extremely difficult for them to risk rejection or criticism. This leads to perfectionist behavior and a high level of self-criticism. As a consequence, they set very high standards for themselves, usually are very responsible and hardworking, and will do anything rather than risk failure in their own eyes or those of their colleagues and friends.

This complex web of emotional traps leads many who suffer in this way to a lifetime of futility. Their overwhelming sense of responsibility for the happiness of others causes their enormous guilt. This message may have been imparted directly by parents, or indirectly by being exposed to the suffering of the parents.

All of these strands lead to an emotionally devastating life. In relationships to self, others, and to work, relationship addicts are slowly spinning into a vortex of emotional, spiritual, and intellectual exhaustion. Small wonder, then, that many find themselves gradually entrapped by other types of addiction discussed above.

# CHAPTER VII

# Key Elements in Recovery

There are several key areas that predict a good outcome for an individual struggling to deal with addiction. Furthermore, it appears that the success of treatment is heavily influenced by the degree to which it encourages the person to be willing to change, agree to detox, to change his environment, to get the right kind of support, to do the work according to plan, and to undertake long-term personal development.

## WILLINGNESS TO CHANGE

One of the best-known books on the subject of alcoholism is *I'll Quit Tomorrow*. I like this title, because it captures one of the great difficulties an individual encounters in the struggle with addiction: the willingness to admit that he has a problem and needs to change. This willingness to change does not imply such complex motivations as doing it in order to become a better person or to heal the damage to oneself or others. These are usually the reasons for *staying* clean and sober, rather than the reasons that bring the person initially to confront his addiction.

For the most part, people in active addiction feel shame and guilt to a great degree and are thus highly unlikely to be driven to recovery by such noble feelings. The reasons that many people contemplate change are practical and immediate. They usually decide to change because their addiction is threatening them with a substantial loss. Losing one's job, one's spouse, one's driving license, one's house, or facing a term in prison, are all common motivations that bring people into the frame of mind where change is contemplated. This type of motivation is called extrinsic motivation, meaning that the desire to change is based on external factors.

Extrinsic motivation is usually sufficient to help a person take the first steps towards recovery. It is very rarely sufficient to keep a person away from his addiction for any length of time, unless it is supplanted by intrinsic motivation. Intrinsic motivation means wanting change in order to be a better person, to parent one's children properly, to be respected, to lead a productive life, and so on. Intrinsic motivation usually grows alongside recovery. An individual who is clean and sober begins to build a different set of values, and operates out of greater self-esteem and a more mature attitude to life.

It doesn't really matter what reason a person has to start recovery, so long as it helps him begin the process. An addicted person might die before more noble reasons for change can emerge. This is useful information for anyone who wants to encourage someone to face up to an addiction. I will discuss this aspect in more detail in the next chapter. The desire to change, extrinsic or intrinsic, is essential to recovery. It is, however, only one strand in the cable of healing addiction, and rarely is sufficient by itself.

## DETOXIFICATION

Detoxification is an important element in long-term healing from addiction. In the more commonly used sense of the word, it refers to a short time in a hospital under sedation, while the body clears out the toxic drugs that the addict has used. That aspect is important and useful for a minority of addicts who are usually in a chronic stage of addiction to mood-altering substances, such as alcohol or heroin. This is not the meaning in which I use it here.

Detoxification, as I use the word, refers to a broader, much neglected aspect of the treatment and care of recovering addicts. Most people in addiction are seriously hindered by the toxins they carry around in their body. These toxins may be a result of a poor diet, lack of proper sleep, and environmental damage, as much as to the drugs themselves. A growing body of evidence shows that our emotional well-being is significantly related to the health of our bodies. When our bodies are unhealthy, it is far more likely that our emotional well-being is easier to undermine.

To this finding we can add a profoundly significant fact: namely, that the strongest predictor of relapse in addiction is a negative emotional state. Thus, it is crucial for recovering addicts to protect their emotional integrity, if they are to stay clean and sober. One of the useful bits of advice that circulates among the Alcoholics Anonymous fellowship is that people need to be alert to their negative states of Hunger, Anger, Loneliness, and Tiredness, or HALT for short. Negative emotional states have many causes and are unavoidable in certain situations. However, when these states are a direct result of a toxic build-up of chemicals in the body, then all the good intentions for sobriety will not help. Such help is available in complementary medicine (sometimes called alternative medicine, which can detoxify the body, and thus negate this potential threat to sobriety.

## CHANGING THE ENVIRONMENT

Everything that people do occurs in a context. Most people have sex on a bed, eat at a table, go to their workplace, wash in the bathroom, and meet friends in pubs or restaurants. For the most part, we are creatures of habit and we like our everyday lives to be somewhat consistent. Addicts are no different—their addiction also happens in a context. This context includes the people they are with, the places they use, the sounds, tastes, and feelings involved in the addictive activity. All of these can trigger the need to act out the addiction. It is extremely difficult for an addicted person to stop his addiction while remaining in his familiar environment.

The effects of environment on addiction cannot be underestimated. Let's look at some of the more telling evidence in this regard. Early in the 1900s, a Russian psychologist discovered that physical reactions not under conscious control can be triggered by circumstances that have no natural connection to those reactions. This information has profound implications for addiction. Pavlov used dogs in his experiments. When presented with food, a dog salivates automatically. When a bell was rung at the same time, the dog's physical system made a connection between the bell and salivating, so that after a certain number of sessions, the dog would salivate at the sound of the bell alone.

The important point here is that the dog did not sit back and think, "Oh, I hear the bell, so the food must be coming, therefore, I must salivate." What actually happens is that the bell—because it is now associated with food in the dog's nervous system—sends certain sound waves that enter the dog's central nervous system and trigger the salivation response. This kind of learning is called conditioning: the dog has been conditioned to salivate when he hears the bell. This conditioning also works in the addictive process. Some examples will help to clarify this point.

During the Vietnam War more and more American soldiers began to use drugs, so that in the later stages of the war a large number of GIs were using heroin regularly. The establishment was concerned that, once the soldiers returned, American society would face a drug problem of unprecedented proportions. Despite all the dire predictions, something very different happened. Of the soldiers who were habitual heroin users, 92 percent stopped using the drug within one year of returning, most of them without any intervention. The remaining 8 percent was the same number of men who had used heroin before they joined the army.

This finding supports the argument that environment plays a huge role in sustaining addiction. A young man who returns from the war to a small farm in the deep South will find it difficult to buy heroin. He does not have to kill people as part of his day job, nor does he fear for his life. His friends down at the local bar are not users, so there is nothing to trigger a craving for the drug. These and many other changes in the environment has made the task of quitting so much easier.

Most people who quit smoking can attest to the power of the environment in triggering the craving for a cigarette. Soon after I had stopped smoking, I was sitting in a hotel having watched my favorite soccer team lose an important game. I was so interested in the game I was reasonably comfortable without a cigarette in my hand. My brother arrived, and we decided to stay and chat. I ordered another pint, we sat down and he rolled a cigarette. As my brother continued talking, his voice seemed to be drifting away, and his cigarette seemed to get bigger and bigger. My conscious mind seemed to be paralyzed, taken over totally by desperately wanting to smoke. Before asking him for a cigarette, I became aware of all the movement and sensations that would occur in taking a drag of a cigarette. I could feel it touching my lips, the slow seductive drawing in of the smoke, the dizzy sensation of the nicotine hit. I took the cigarette, lit it, and it felt great. That was my last nicotine fix. (At least so far.)

Heroin addicts who are released from prison detoxified and drug free, can—often for years—experience an almost overwhelming desire to use the moment they find themselves in a familiar place where drug use is occurring. What is of great interest is that their brain chemistry reacts as if it had a heroin fix, even when there is no drug present. Some of the treatments for addiction involve getting addicts to handle needles and the other accoutrements consistently without shooting up, as a way of retraining their bodies from the expectation that sets off the craving for the drug.

Many alcoholics can recount going into a bar and waking up several days later wondering what happened. These experiences have led some people to suggest that addicts are out of control. A more accurate view is that the individual is being unconsciously controlled by subtle but powerful cues that are setting off the addictive process. Part of my own work with recovering addicts involves helping them deal with their relapses, or slips. I have yet to find that a relapse happens with no precipitating cause, and almost always there is some environmental impact that facilitates the relapse. In many cases, the individual is unaware of the forces that were at work leading up to the relapse.

All these accounts as well as recent research suggest that long-term recovery requires an understanding of environmental effects. In other words, the addicted person needs to become aware of the kinds of experiences—such as the tastes, smells, sounds, interactions, people and situations—that may lead him back to addiction. There are no hard-and-fast rules that will fit everybody, and there are limits to how much change a person can make. That said, some changes to a person's environment are almost always necessary in recovery. I will give some specific guidelines in the next chapter.

## GETTING THE RIGHT KIND OF SUPPORT

Very few people can make significant changes in their lives without the support or influence of others. Even the most resolutely independent people, who believe they made their important decisions and life changes without recourse to others, have in general been influenced by those around them. It is logical to accept the fact that dealing with an addiction goes more smoothly if friends and family help by being positive influences. Addicts who spurn the help of others have a poorer prognosis than those who can ask for and receive help and encouragement.

The key issue here is the right kind of support. A doctor who himself is an alcoholic is unlikely to give the needed support to someone with a drinking problem. A food-addicted parent is less likely to help his or her anorexic daughter. A drug-dependent psychiatrist is less likely to confront a tranquilizer addict. Those people who have an active addiction problem will be of little support to someone trying to recover. Rather, they will be more inclined to aid and abet the denial of other addicts, by minimizing the problem or explaining it away.

Where, then, does a person get the right kind of support? The supporting person must care for the welfare of the addicted person and must also know something about addiction. A caring spouse who becomes knowledgeable about the basic needs of recovering addicts can be as important in helping the healing process along as a professional counselor or a member of a support group. The people who are probably most useful in giving support are those who are also in recovery and attend recovery groups, including the twelve-step programs. The success of these programs is significantly related to the fellowship and support that the members provide for each other.

## WORKING TO A PLAN

One of the defining characteristics of many addictions is that they lead a person into a life that becomes chaotic and unmanageable. The individual's emotional life is topsy-turvy, and he often feels as if he is on an emotional roller coaster. Finances are often affected, leading to worry and insecurity. Relationships suffer and lack consistency. In the early months of recovery, the work goes best if there is a plan that the individual can use to put structure and predictability into his day-to-day living. Addicts often have great difficulty tolerating boredom and ordinariness. A person has to learn a degree of such tolerance—it is part of a healthy life. Constantly looking for a high, a buzz, or a fix is not a healthy path to recovery.

My father once used a phrase that comes to mind. He was discussing how to cope with difficulty, and advised me that I should learn how to "do the menial task." As the years passed, I have grown to see the wisdom in this approach. Sometimes during distress and difficulty, it is a great help to have some predictable task in which to involve oneself.

Working with a plan means designing a fairly rigid timetable of events that include work, recreational exercises, and recovery activities. Such a plan can be built around other elements I have discussed above and could include activities such as changing the environment, adopting new hobbies and interests, getting support through new friends or in support meetings, and so on. A counselor or support person may help the addict design such a plan. Consistent effort to stay with the plan and also to shape it to suit special needs helps the individual achieve some sense of order in his life and cope with many of the insecurities and difficulties involved in early recovery.

## UNDERTAKING LONG-TERM PERSONAL DEVELOPMENT

It is clear that recovery is not simply a matter of stopping an addictive activity. It also involves making fundamental changes in one's lifestyle and habit patterns. In order to proceed through the changes necessary to live well and healthily without recourse to addictive behavior, most people require a long-term program of personal development. Otherwise, people may kick one addictive habit only to find themselves continually frustrated, craving the addictive substance, or simply replacing it with some other addiction.

Central to this argument is understanding that addiction masks personal difficulties and prevents people from maturing and leading an emotionally healthy life. When the addiction is no longer active, the individual still has to face all the problems he avoided through addiction. For example, people who begin drinking heavily in late adolescence live through their twenties and thirties in a fog of alcohol, and as a result did not grow through the developmental stages of early adulthood. When they stop drinking, many are not mature—they are still adolescents psychologically. In order to catch up to their actual age—middle adulthood with its wisdom and responsibilities—they may need some guidance and counseling.

Commitment to long-term development is a crucial aspect of recovery. We have seen earlier that every person's addiction has a particular meaning and is used for a particular purpose. These meanings and purposes may in fact be of real value. Spiritual experiences, peace of mind, avoidance of suffering are in themselves important. It is the use of addiction to achieve these ends that is destructive. Unless the individual discovers the meaning and purpose of the addiction, and finds new ways of achieving these purposes, he will probably relapse, break down, or live in chronic, low-level misery.

# CHAPTER VIII

# How to Get the Help You Need

Most people think that the helping professions are a group of people who hope to do the best they can for the good of humanity. Within the field of addiction, one might hope this view to predominate—compassionate, intelligent people, striving toward a common goal of helping addicts to recover. What a pity this view does not reflect reality. Over the past fifty years or so, the field of addiction study and treatment has been marked by political infighting.

Central to the problems in the helping professions is the belief that there is only one true answer to the problem of addiction. Different approaches have one thing in common: they have all asserted at some time or another that their view was the "truth."

There is an old adage that "when doctors differ, patients die." This is certainly true where addiction is concerned—many people have died because the professionals were too busy trying to prove the truth of their particular model, rather than seeking new, creative approaches to treatment. The "truth" is that there are several approaches to the treatment of addiction; each of these works well for certain people and not so well for others. Different treatments have different success rates; no single one works for everybody. However, most will work better than no treatment at all.

I will briefly examine the major options available to someone with an addiction who wants help: medication, twelve-step support groups, individual or group counseling, hospital-based services, residential treatment in a specialist treatment center, addiction rehabilitation centers, and what I call the do-it-yourself approach. Each type of treatment has its strengths and weaknesses, and each to some extent carries assumptions about the nature of addiction. In most cases of addiction, I recommend that a person find a suitable mix of options that best suits their temperament and life situation.

Before discussing these options, here is some brief guidance for people who are concerned about someone who is addicted. In general such people are the spouses, parents, family members, friends, or colleagues of someone whose life is being damaged by drugs, alcohol, or some other addiction.

## GUIDELINES FOR THOSE WHO CARE

Many people spend enormous energy and are saddened and become emotionally damaged in their fruitless efforts to help someone in addiction. They lack the insight needed to deal with this problem effectively. Instead, they rely on ordinary common sense and their optimistic belief in the force of reason and of love.

Two priorities are essential for a healthy approach to addiction: the persons who care must protect themselves and get the addict to seek help. Here's a list of suggestions.

1.  Get assistance from an addiction counselor—even one or two sessions can be a great help.

2. Join a support group, like Al Anon or Nar Anon, for those people whose lives are affected by their relationship with an addicted person. You will need help and support in order to operate in the ways presented below.

3. Learn about addiction through reading and discussion.

4. Do not enable the addict. Do not prevent him from experiencing the consequences of his addiction. Do not cover up for him, or make excuses on his behalf.

5. Do not discuss the problem with him while he is under the influence.

6. Do not nag, manipulate, ridicule, snipe at, demean, or attack the addict.

7. If you are threatened, attacked, or in danger, get out of the house and report it to the police.

8. Do not lend the addict money for the addictive substance or activity.

9. Tell the addict that you are concerned and believe that he needs help. Do this once or twice, then leave it alone. Do not deliver this message in an angry or sarcastic way, or at an inappropriate time.

10. If the addict does not get help, plan to leave, or to ask the person to leave. Living with an addict who refuses to acknowledge the problem is a short road to a life full of chronic misery and serious emotional damage. Staying with the addict will prolong the problems, create havoc with your children's emotional development, and give him a false sense of security.

11. Do not make threats that you will not or cannot carry out. This destroys your credibility.

12. Always remember that you cannot change another person, but if you yourself change, the addict may choose to change in response.

13. Do not keep the problem a secret—it will end up destroying you emotionally.

14. Recognize the normal rules of reason and moral conscience are damaged in the addict. What you *do* will be far more effective than what you *say*.

You will be far more effective once you begin to use the above guidelines. He will then have to come to terms much more quickly with the necessity of getting help. The following is a description of the kinds of help available.

## MEDICATION

The use of medication to assist in the treatment of addiction has a very questionable history. Most of the drugs used to treat addiction are themselves addictive. We have seen earlier the devastating effects of using heroin to treat opium addiction and cocaine to treat morphine addiction. It is important to distinguish between a harm reduction approach and a treatment approach to addiction.

The use of methadone for heroin addicts is a good example of harm reduction. Methadone is a highly toxic, addictive substance that is given under medical supervision to heroin addicts. The purpose is to help the heroin user minimize the risk of disease through dirty needles and to prevent him from resorting to crime in order to get money to feed his habit.

Such approaches are important from a social and legal viewpoint. There is a tacit acceptance here that some people who are addicted to heroin are going to stay actively addicted, no matter what is done to help them. It is not the function of this book to argue the effectiveness of this approach. I include it here in order to clarify the fact that reducing the harm associated with some addictions is not a treatment for the addiction itself. Methadone is not a treatment for heroin addiction.

Because of the recent interest in the biochemistry of addiction, we see a new emphasis on drug therapy as a direct treatment for addiction. The assumption underlying this approach is that addicts are suffering from a biochemical imbalance that causes their addiction. More specifically, there is recent research on the levels of dopamine and serotonin in the brains of addicts, no matter whether they are alcoholics, gamblers, sex addicts, or anorexics. I am very skeptical about this approach to addiction. I believe that it is, in part, an effort by the medical profession to provide an explanation—as well as to gain control of treatment—for what is an enormous social problem.

There is a precedent for this. In the 1930s and 1940s, it became clear that the moral or religious approaches to alcohol abuse were not working, and that the twelve-step approach, which saw alcoholism as a distinct progressive disease, had much to offer (one of the founder members of AA was a medical doctor). This approach was embraced by the medical establishment and, as a result, it gained control of state funding on the one hand and payment by health insurers on the other for the medical treatment of alcoholism. The amounts of money involved are enormous.

It is understandable that the medical approach to alcoholism prevailed because so little was understood about addiction at the time. Now, however, far more information is available, and it is clear that, despite the vast expenditure by medical and psychiatric services, alcoholism has not been shown to be a disease entity in the medical use of the word; nor does the most successful treatment of alcohol abuse involve medicine. I think it is important to learn from these historical precedents when the treatment of addiction is in question.

If medication is offered to someone in the grip of addiction, it is either seen as a method of harm reduction and as such may have some benefit; or it is a direct effort at treating the addiction. If it is seen as a treatment, serious questions remain as to whether the assumptions underlying this approach are correct. Treating gamblers or anorexics with Prozac or a similar medication may take the focus off what is really going on in their addiction. It is a simple, neat philosophy that to my mind is very premature and perhaps misleading. There may be a role for medication in a small percentage of cases. In general, however, I believe it is best to await further support before embracing this treatment.

Medication is also used as a means of counteracting the effects of the addictive substance, or making the person feel ill if taken in conjunction with the substance. A good example of the former is the use of Naloxone, which prevents the heroin user from experiencing the pleasant effects of heroin. The drug Disulfuram (antabuse) is an example of the latter, which makes the alcoholic very sick if he drinks an alcoholic beverage while antabuse is present in his system. These two drugs do not treat addiction; they make addiction uncomfortable, or prevent the drug from taking effect. They have some benefit if taken by a highly motivated individual as a stopgap to avoid relapse.

## TWELVE-STEP PROGRAMS

One of the most significant developments in addiction treatment began in the 1930s with the twelve-step program of Alcoholics Anonymous. This program was developed over a period of years by two individuals—both serious alcohol abusers—a businessman named Bill Wilson and a doctor named Bob Smith. In their joint search for a way to recover from alcoholism, they devised a program based on their own experiences, which also incorporated the spiritual psychology of Carl Jung, the writings of William James, and the then current Christian evangelical renewal.

In the decades since then, the program has developed and proliferated, and is now used as a basic model of recovery for a wide variety of addictions. These include gambling, drug addiction, eating disorders and relationship difficulties with addicts of one sort of another. Twelve-step programs have been enormously beneficial and to date have helped hundreds of thousands of people find their way back to sobriety and health.

There are several reasons for the success of this model. Those who partake regularly in the meetings are helped in three ways.

1. The program is acknowledged as spiritual in nature, and the first step is concerned with the individual's recognition and acceptance of becoming powerless over a substance or activity. This has the effect of encouraging the addict's willingness to change, a key element in recovery. Addiction occurs when people give themselves up or over to the addictive substance or activity—it then takes control of their lives and eventually destroys them if they do not find recovery. The twelve-step program acknowledges this, and

provides the possibility for the individual to support his recovery by giving himself up or over to something else, a higher power, and to the program itself. This can have a remarkably healing power.

2. The recovering individual is influenced and supported by the fellowship of others in a similar position. The encouragement and, more crucially, the sense of identification, found among fellow members form a very positive basis for continuing sobriety. Added to this is what is called sponsorship, whereby an individual with a long period of sobriety takes the role of sponsor (or mentor) with a newly recovering addict. The healthy example provided, as well as the advice and support, has often helped a new member from returning to addiction in moments of crisis.

3. A change of environment and lifestyle (crucial elements in recovering from addiction) is made possible by partaking in the program. Most addicts have consistent, habitual ways of acting out their addiction. Frequenting particular pubs or betting shops, and consorting with a set of equally sick companions make it very difficult for them to cease their addiction.

Being part of a fellowship provides new avenues for friendship and different recreational patterns—the bowling alley and coffee mornings replace the card table and the pub. Additionally, twelve-step meetings are easily accessible and are free. Anyone struggling in addiction who wants help would be well advised to give them a try.

Twelve-step programs have some limitations. When an addiction grows out of the pain of a damaged, hurt person, the program—while helping that person stay sober and learn a new way of living—will not be able to address his deeper needs for healing. Rather, the person may keep clear of the primary addiction, only to find himself addicted to something new, including perhaps an addiction to the fellowship itself. This is shown in the numbers of people who spend decades in the fellowship, but seem to go around in circles, continually telling the same old stories and showing little in the quality of their lives that suggests they are getting any better.

For a significant number of recovering addicts, much of the damage to their personalities will have been covered up through addiction and is often outside their conscious awareness. It may take some period in counseling combined with continued involvement in the fellowship to make a difference.

Another limitation of the program is that some people find the spiritual emphasis very difficult to embrace. Those who use the program have already absorbed a particular version of the spiritual way of life, and there is in some cases a certain arrogance that exists in any ideologically based group.

Those who don't succeed and find no other help will usually die, and their voices are left unheard. Why they could not benefit from the program, or what the blocks were that prevented them from healing, is left unknown.

With these qualifications, we can still acknowledge that twelve-step programs are a very powerful and effective source of healing and recovery for many people. I do not, however, believe that they are the only way to health and sobriety.

## ADDICTION TREATMENT CENTERS

Residential treatment for addiction has become very common in the past twenty-five years. The Minnesota Model was born out of the twelve-step movement, when a group of recovering alcoholics set up a center to encourage others to join them in a peaceful setting away from their usual environment. The treatment usually involves a four- to six-week residential program that combines the twelve-step approach with other forms of counseling and group therapy.

One of the major advantages of a treatment center is this: those who care about and are worried about the addict can get help through these agencies and learn how to deal with the addict differently, so as to encourage his entry into treatment. By making contact with a treatment center, an individual can be told how to encourage the addict to get into treatment. This means that the addict may get into recovery faster than if he is left to "bottom out" and join a program of his own accord.

Treatment centers vary in their success rates. Anyone close to the issue of addiction realizes that there will be a percentage of addicts who will not recover, no matter what happens to them. The decision to undertake treatment for addiction at a treatment center is a difficult one for many people. In general, if after trying a twelve-step program and after listening to the advice of professionals familiar with the problem of addiction, an individual is still unable to abstain or control his habit, a treatment center may be the best option.

The strengths of a good residential treatment center can complement the twelve-step program in the following ways. It takes the person out of his usual environment and provides him with a drug- or activity-free context in which to take stock of his life. It provides support by and identification with the other members of the treatment group. It provides counseling and education that help speed up his self-understanding. Most importantly, it provides weekly after-care group meetings once the individual has successfully completed the residential period of treatment.

## COUNSELING

The field of counseling and psychotherapy has been criticized for its approach to addiction, and much of this criticism is justified. Many counselors who are schooled in the classical therapy models of psychoanalysis, or in cognitive therapy, or other therapies, do not have specific training in the field of addiction. They tend to use their therapeutic approach inappropriately, in the belief that addiction responds to therapy the same way other human problems do. This is not the case. Nor is their widespread notion that addiction is simply a symptom of other psychological problems. As a result, many active addicts— especially those with problems—spend their time going from one therapist or psychiatrist to another often for years, trying to sort out all their psychological problems. In truth, there is no hope of recovery for these people until their addiction is addressed. Because of their training and ideological stance, the best-intentioned and most skillful therapists may miss this essential point.

More recent developments in the field of counseling have focused on the specific problems associated with addiction. There is now a branch of counseling devoted specifically to addiction, and some counselors specialize in this field. They are known as addiction counselors and are, at least initially, a better option for someone with an addiction problem. I say initially because, in my opinion, there is a problem in the training of counselors. On its own, the training is too narrow in focus. While addiction should not be reduced to another problem and needs to have specific therapeutic efforts addressed to its nature and its place in a person's life, neither can it be separated completely from many of the other aspects of the person's psychological and spiritual nature. Thus, for long-term recovery, I believe that counseling is best provided by someone who has in-depth experience and training in many aspects of human psychology, but who also has specific exposure to addiction and its treatment.

## HOSPITAL-BASED TREATMENT

State and private health services are being expanded to deal with addicts. This is in response to the growing incidence of addiction problems, and to the fact that addiction is being recognized now as a specific health problem in its own right. Consequently, more and more hospitals offer services to addicts. Their focus is still primarily on the treatment of alcoholism, because it continues to be the most destructive and widespread addiction in the United States.

Hospital-based services are varied. Some provide detoxification and include a short residential program. Others place emphasis on an out-patient program that incorporates group therapy, individual counseling, and rehabilitation activities. Some encourage patients to attend a twelve-step program such as Alcoholics Anonymous. Others favor retraining the patient so that he is able to control his substance use.

There is continued expansion of these services, and the focus appears to be moving away from residential treatment towards outpatient care. There are strengths in this approach. It is more accessible to a larger number of people and perhaps can reach a person in early-stage addiction. Such a person is, in my opinion, far more likely to visit an outpatient counseling service, than to sign in for a six-week intensive residential program. On the other hand, the outpatient approach can place a very heavy burden on some patients who have no respite from the environmental cues that trigger their addiction. For some addicts these problems and environmental triggers feel insurmountable, and they might do better taking a break away from their everyday environment until some recovery work has had a chance to take hold.

## REHABILITATION CENTERS

These differ from the treatment centers described above in that their focus is on long-term rehabilitation, rather than on short-term, intensive treatment. Clients tend to stay for periods up to a year. Rehabilitation centers provide individuals with a safe environment and a support network while they try to rebuild their lives. They are encouraged to forge links with the community through work and socially. Participants live at the center and take responsibility for day-to-day domestic tasks, thus re-learning, in many cases, the basic skills of looking after themselves and of taking responsibility for their lives. Participants are expected to partake in a twelve-step program as a central part of their recovery.

These centers do not use the intensive therapy found in a residential program. Many people who use these centers could not afford to get private treatment. Many are deprived because of their addiction, but also through the very real social impoverishment that is often a major causal factor in the development of addiction. In general, the average stay at such a center ranges from several months to a year.

## THE DO-IT-YOURSELF APPROACH

We have seen earlier that very few people achieve anything of significance in their lives solely on their own. Inability to trust, a strong ego, or fundamental insecurity often lead people to believe that they are more independent than they actually are. That said, some people are more independent than others—it is simply a matter of degree. Those more independent types who also have an addiction problem may be attracted to the notion that they will beat their addiction on their own.

A good example of this approach is the millions of people who succeed in giving up smoking. Of all addictions, cigarette smoking is one of the most endemic and difficult to beat.

The do-it-yourself approach is defined here as quitting an addiction without engaging professional help or joining a recovery program. While it is a path fraught with difficulty, it is possible for some people to succeed. Certain addictions are also more accessible to this approach than others.

The following is some strategic advice, based on the key elements of recovery discussed in the previous chapter.

### Prepare to Stop

This stage involves preparing one's mind for the day you will quit. Take a month to do this. During this period, read some books on the topic of addiction. List reasons for stopping, and program your mind by repeating some of these reasons every day. Set a definite target date for stopping, and tell your friends your decision.

### Change the Way and Amount You Use

During the preparation stage, start cutting down, but do not let yourself be seduced into the notion that you will gradually cut out the habit. Use the cutting-down period to strengthen your resolve to stop completely. Tell yourself that it will help lessen withdrawal when D-Day arrives. Cutting down means using less, so postpone the first dose, or take it later than usual. Set an upper limit each day.

Change the setting in which you use your drug, by making it less pleasant. If you like using it in company, then do it alone. Break the triggers by avoiding use of your drug in more pleasant surroundings. Acknowledge that you are an addict, and try to take any romance out of being an addict. Set up a more active schedule of activities, particularly those that have no connection to your drug use, such as evening classes, hobbies, or charity work.

## D-Day

On the day you quit, remind yourself of the following:

- Quitting is possible, and thousands of people do it successfully.

- You owe it to yourself not to be a slave to a substance, or activity.

- Withdrawal symptoms are temporary and will ease soon.

- If you relapse, you have to start all over again.

- One use of your drug of choice will lead to another use of it.

- For someone who has an addiction problem, there is no such thing as one drink, cigarette, bet, or fix. This is a very important affirmation, because the temptation is almost always couched in terms of "just one."

- Write the above advice on an index card, carry it around, and read it every hour.

Do the following:

- Each day, tell someone that you have stayed clean.

- Do not lie.

- Use a relaxation method, such as breathing exercises, to music each morning.

- Stay away from tempting environments.

- Review your list of reasons for wanting to quit.

- Talk about non-use to friends and relatives, and enlist their support.

- Distract yourself by doing something during a craving experience, rather than analyzing your feelings.

- If you slip, do not use it as an excuse for complete relapse.

- Get some physical exercise each day.

This do-it-yourself approach does not address the causes for addiction; nor does it address the void that is often left in the life of a recovering addict. It is presented here as a simple guide to those who wish to try it. In my own experience, it will work for some, but many do better in a more structured approach. It can, however, be incorporated into an individual's use of other resources—such as following a twelve-step program or getting counseling—and is perhaps best used in that context.

# Index

projecting, 25
anorexia. see also bulimia; eating disorders
  described, 68-70
  drug therapy for, 95
  rationalization of, 23
anorexic behavior, 31
antabuse, 95
antidepressant addiction, 52
antidepressants
  discussed, 50-52
  MAOIs, 51
  SSRIs, 51
  tricyclics, 51
antifreeze, 63
anxiety. see also emotions
  alcoholic, 40
  drug-induced, 15, 20
  drug-suppressed, 45-48
  relief from, 13
apocalypse, expectations for, 20
appetite suppressants, 48. see also amphetamines
Argentina, 69
Aronson, Eliot, 20
aspirin, 44
asthma, 48
Ativan, 45
attention deficit disorder (ADD), 48, 73
attitude. see also spirituality
  relation to drug use, 58

**B**
banisteriopsis, 57
behavior changes. see also personality changes
  as danger sign, 30-31
Benzedrine, 49
benzodiazepines, 45
beta-blockers, 46
boredom, 87
brain function. see also alcoholism
  chemicals affecting, 35-37, 54-56

psychological forces affecting, 36-37, 64
breathing exercises, 16, 105
British Medical Journal, 38
Brompton Cocktail, 61
bulimia. see also anorexia; eating disorders
  discussed, 68-70

**C**
caffeine, 63
cannabis. see marijuana
caregiver guidelines, discussed, 91-93
cerebral cortex, 35-36, 49
chasing the dragon, 18
  discussed, 26-27
chemical dependence, described, 35-37
child abuse, 38. see also violence
childhood experiences. see also adolescents; infancy
  role in addiction, 14, 78
China, 73
chocolate, 66-67
cocaine
  compared to amphetamines, 48
  crack cocaine, 60, 61
  effects of, 15-16, 60, 61, 93
cocaine addiction
  discussed, 61-63
  drug therapy for, 17
codeine, 53
cognitive dissonance, 20
complementary medicine, 82
compulsion, 8, 9
computer games, 72
conditioning, 83-84
confidence
  drug-induced feelings of, 13
  projecting, 25
connection, drug-induced feelings of, 13
cough, 34
counseling, 91, 99. see also help resources

powerlessness, causes and characteristics of, 15
prescription drugs. see also specific drugs
  discussed, 44-45
pride, 75
projection, described, 24-26
Prozac, 51, 95
psilocybin, 57
psychological addiction. see also addiction
  addictive relationships, 77-79
  eating disorders, 66-70
  gambling, 64-66
  in general, 65
  religiosity, 75-77
  sex addiction, 73-74
  shopping, 70-71
  television, 71-73
  work addiction, 74-75
psychostimulants. see also amphetamines
  discussed, 60-61

**Q**
Quaaludes, 49
quitting. see also help resources; withdrawal
  guidelines for, 102-105

**R**
rationalization, 65
  described, 22-23
rave generation, 60
reality
  altering, 16, 56-57
  suppressing, 21, 76-77
recovery elements. see also help resources
  detoxification, 81-82
  environmental change, 83-86
  long-term personal development, 88-89
  support requirements, 86-87
  willingness to change, 80-81
  working to plan, 87-88

regularity, 8, 9, 32-33
rehabilitation centers, described, 102
relapse, 85, 89
relationships. see also addictive relationships
  destructive, 15
  deterioration of, 41
  with substances, 40
relaxation exercises, 105
religiosity. see also spirituality
  discussed, 75-77
resentment, 25-26
responsibility
  accepting, 9, 18, 25-26
  guilt and, 79
Ritalin, 48
Rolling Stones, 47
Royhypnol, 45

**S**
schizophrenia, 50, 51
secrecy, 93
self-control, loss of, 37-38
self-esteem, 77-78, 81
self-mutilation, 14
serotonin, 49, 51, 52, 61
Seroxat, 51
sex addiction, discussed, 73-74
sexuality, 35, 60, 63
shame, 80
shopping, discussed, 70-71
sleep patterns, 40, 52
Smith, Bob, 96
smoking. see also nicotine
  addiction to, 84, 103
  deaths from, 43
soap operas, 72
social values, role in addictive behavior, 16-17, 37-38
society, addict as danger to, 38
solvents, 63
speed. see amphetamine
spirituality. see also altered states of consciousness; religiosity
  drug use and, 16-17, 56, 89

To receive a current catalog from The Crossing Press
please call toll-free, 800-777-1048.
Visit our Web site: **www.crossingpress.com**